Capital Budgeting

Steven M. Bragg

AccountingTools®

Published by AccountingTools, Inc., Centennial, Colorado.

ISBN 978-1-64221-293-8

For more information about AccountingTools® products, visit our Web site at www.accountingtools.com.

Printed in the United States of America

Table of Contents

About the Author

Steven Bragg, CPA, has been the chief financial officer or controller of four companies, as well as a consulting manager at Ernst & Young. He received a master's degree in finance from Bentley College, an MBA from Babson College, and a Bachelor's degree in Economics from the University of Maine. He has been a two-time president of the Colorado Mountain Club, and is an avid alpine skier, mountain biker, and certified master diver. Mr. Bragg resides in Centennial, Colorado. He has written more than 300 books and courses, including *New Controller Guidebook*, *GAAP Guidebook*, and *Payroll Management*.

Steven maintains the accountingtools.com web site, which contains continuing professional education courses, the Accounting Best Practices podcast, and thousands of articles on accounting subjects.

Buy Additional AccountingTools Courses

AccountingTools offers more than 1,500 hours of CPE courses, with concentrations in accounting, auditing, finance, taxation, and ethics. Related courses that you might like include:

- Budgeting
- Business Strategy
- Fixed Asset Accounting
- Fixed Asset Controls
- How to Audit Fixed Assets
- Project Accounting
- Project Management

Go to accountingtools.com/cpe to view these additional courses.

AccountingTools®

Chapter 1
Overview of Capital Budgeting

Introduction

One of the most significant debates that the management team of a business can engage in is whether to spend funds on capital items or other activities. These capital items may involve (for example) increases in the productive capacity of a business, an investment in a new corporate headquarters, or perhaps a government-mandated installation of pollution controls. Some investments may be of a more short-term nature and not even involve fixed assets, such as investments in a marketing campaign, product research, or employee training. There may be dozens or even hundreds of prospective investment proposals being forwarded from all over a business. The typical organization will have varying amounts of cash available to invest in these items, so the management team must have a system for determining which investments to make and which to avoid. This system is called *capital budgeting*.

Before a business expends funds on investment proposals, it must evaluate whether funds should be committed; this may include an analysis of the costs, related benefits, and impact on capacity levels of the prospective purchase. In this chapter, we describe several issues to consider when deciding whether to make a capital investment.

> **Related Podcast Episodes:** Episodes 144 and 145 of the Accounting Best Practices Podcast discuss evaluating capital expenditure proposals and capital expenditures with minimal cash, respectively. They are available at: **accountingtools.com/podcasts** or **iTunes**

Overview of Capital Budgeting

The normal capital expenditure analysis process is for the management team to request investment proposals from all parts of the company. Managers respond by filling out a standard request form, outlining what they want to buy and how it will benefit the company. An analyst then reviews these proposals to determine which are worthy of an investment, after which management decides which proposals to accept. Any proposals that are accepted are included in the annual budget, and will be purchased during the next budget year. Fixed assets purchased in this manner also require a certain number of approvals, with more approvals required by increasingly senior levels of management if the sums involved are substantial.

Management needs a method for ranking the priority of projects, so that funds are assigned to the most deserving projects. The traditional method for doing so is net present value (NPV) analysis, which focuses on picking proposals with the largest amount of discounted cash flows. This concept is addressed in the Discounted Cash Flow Analysis chapter.

The trouble with NPV analysis is that it does not account for how an investment might impact the profit generated by the entire system of production; instead, it tends to favor the optimization of specific work centers, which may have no particular impact on overall profitability. Also, the results of NPV are based on the future projections of cash flows, which may be wildly inaccurate. Given these concerns, we describe constraint analysis in the Constraint Analysis chapter. This analysis focuses on how to maximize use of the bottleneck operation. The bottleneck operation is the most constricted operation in a company; to improve the overall profitability of the company, concentrate all attention on management of that bottleneck. This has a profound impact on capital expenditures, since a proposal should have some favorable impact on that operation in order to be approved.

There are two scenarios under which certain project proposals may avoid any kind of cash flow or bottleneck analysis. The first is a legal requirement to install an item. The prime example is environmental equipment, such as smokestack scrubbers, that are mandated by the government. In such cases, there may be some analysis to see if costs can be lowered, but the proposal *must* be accepted, so it will sidestep the normal analysis process.

The second scenario is when a company wants to mitigate a high-risk situation that could imperil the company. In this case, the emphasis is not on profitability at all, but rather on the avoidance of a situation. If so, the mandate likely comes from top management, so there is little additional need for analysis, other than a review to ensure that the lowest-cost alternative is selected.

A final scenario is when there is a sudden need for a fixed asset, perhaps due to the catastrophic failure of existing equipment or a strategic shift. These purchases can happen at any time, and so usually fall outside of the annual capital expenditure planning cycle. It is generally best to require more than the normal number of approvals for these items, so that management is made fully aware of the situation. Also, if there is time to do so, they are worthy of an unusually intense analysis, to see if they really must be purchased at once, or if they can be delayed until the next capital expenditure approval period arrives.

Once all items are properly approved and inserted into the annual budget, this does not end the review process. There is a final review just prior to actually making each purchase, with appropriate approval, to ensure that the company still needs each fixed asset.

The last step in the capital budgeting process is to conduct a post-implementation review, in which is summarized the actual costs and benefits of each fixed asset, with a comparison of these results to the initial projections included in the original application. If the results are worse than expected, this may result in a more in-depth review, with particular attention being paid to avoiding any faulty aspects of the original proposal in future proposals.

The Capital Budgeting Application Form

Most companies require managers to fill out a standardized form for all capital budgeting proposals. The type of information included in the form will vary, depending on whether the approval decision is based on bottleneck considerations or the results of a net present value analysis. However, the header section of the form will likely be the same in all circumstances. It identifies the project, its sponsor, the date on which it was submitted, and a unique project identification number that is filled in by the recipient. A sample header appears in the following exhibit.

Sample Application Header

Project name:	50 ton plastic injection molder
Project sponsor:	E. R. Eddison
Submission date:	May 28 Project number: 2025-10

If a proposal is for a legal requirement or a risk mitigation issue, then it is absolved from most analysis, and will likely move to the top of the approved project list. Consequently, the form should contain a separate section for these types of projects, and should involve a different set of approvers. The corporate attorney may be involved, as well as anyone involved in risk management. A sample block in the application form for legal and risk mitigation issues appears in the following exhibit.

Sample Legal and Risk Mitigation Block

		Required Approvals	
Initial cash flow:	-$250,000	All proposals	*Susan Lafferty*
Year 1 cash flow:	-10,000		Attorney
Year 2 cash flow:	-10,000		
Year 3 cash flow:	-10,000	< $100,000	*George Mason*
			Risk Officer
Describe legal or risk mitigation issue:			
Replanting of pine forest on southern property, with annual forestry review, per new zoning requirements		$100,000+	*Fred Scurry*
			President

If you elect to focus on bottleneck considerations for capital budgeting approvals, then include the following block of text in the application form. This block focuses on the changes in cash flow that are associated with a capital expenditure. The block requests an itemization of the cash flows involved in the purchase (primarily for finance planning considerations), followed by requests for information about how the investment will help the company – via an improvement in throughput, a reduction in operating costs, or an increase in the return on investment. These concepts are explained in the Constraint Analysis chapter.

Sample Bottleneck Approval Block

			Required Approvals
Initial cash flow:	-$125,000	All proposals	*Monica Byers*
Year 1 cash flow:	-8,000		Process Analyst
Year 2 cash flow:	-8,000		
Year 3 cash flow:	-8,000	< $100,000	*Al Rogers*
			Responsible Supervisor
Net throughput change:*	+$180,000		
		$100,000+	*Fred Scurry*
Net operating cost change:*	+$8,000		President
Change in ROI:*	+0.08%		

* On an annual basis

In the example, observe that the primary improvement used as the basis for the proposal is the improvement in throughput. This also leads to an enhancement of the return on investment. There is an increase in the total net operating cost, which represents a reduction in the positive effect of the throughput, and which is caused by the annual $8,000 maintenance cost associated with the investment.

The approvals for a bottleneck-related investment change from the ones shown previously for a legal or risk mitigation investment. In this case, a process analyst should verify the information included in the block, to ensure that the applicant's claims are correct. The supervisor in whose area of responsibility the investment falls should also sign off, thereby accepting responsibility for the outcome of the investment. A higher-level manager, or even the board of directors, should approve any really large investment proposals.

If you do not choose to use a bottleneck-oriented application, then the following block may be useful in the application. It is based on the more traditional analysis of net present value. Also consider using this block as a supplement to the bottleneck block just noted, in case some managers prefer to work with both sets of information.

Sample Net Present Value Information Block

Year	Cash Out (payments)	Cash In (Revenue)	Incremental Tax Effect	Totals
0	-$1,000,000			-$1,000,000
1	-25,000	+$200,000	+$8,750	+183,750
2	-25,000	+400,000	-61,250	+313,750
3	-25,000	+400,000	-61,250	+313,750
4	-25,000	+400,000	-61,250	+313,750
5	-25,000	+400,000	-61,250	+313,750
To-tals	-$1,125,000	+$1,800,000	-$236,250	+$438,750
			Tax Rate:	35%
			Hurdle Rate:	12%
			Net Present Value:	+$13,328

The net present value block requires the presentation of cash flows over a five-year period, as well as the net tax effect resulting from this specific transaction. The tax effect is based on $25,000 of maintenance expenses in every year shown, as well as $200,000 of annual depreciation, and a 35% incremental tax rate. Thus, in Year 2, there is $400,000 of revenue, less $225,000 of depreciation and maintenance expenses, multiplied by 35%, resulting in an incremental tax effect of $61,250. These issues are discussed further in the Discounted Cash Flow Analysis chapter.

The block then goes on to state the corporate hurdle rate, which is 12% in the example. We then discount the stream of cash flows from the project at the hurdle rate of 12%, which results in a positive net present value of $13,328. Based on just the net present value analysis, this appears to be an acceptable project.

A variation on the rather involved text just shown is to shift the detailed cash flow analysis to a backup document, and only show the resulting net present value in the application form.

The text blocks shown here contain much of the key information that management should see before it decides whether to approve a capital investment. In addition, there should be a considerable amount of supporting information that precisely describes the nature of the proposed investment, as well as backup information that supports each number included in the form.

The following sample capital request form shows how it can be structured, though it may need to be modified to meet the specific needs of a business. This form is typically treated as a cover page, with additional analyses attached that may cover a number of additional pages.

Sample Capital Request Application

Capital Request Form

Project Name	Project Number

Project Sponsor	Sponsor Contact Information	Submission Date

Project Type

☐ Constraint improvement ☐ Risk reduction

☐ Cost reduction ☐ Scheduled equipment replacement

☐ Environmental/legal requirement ☐ Other

Project Description

Description Block

Financial Summary

Year 1 Revenue	-	Year 1 Expenses	=	Year 1 Cash Flow
Year 2 Revenue	-	Year 2 Expenses	=	Year 2 Cash Flow
Year 3 Revenue	-	Year 3 Expenses	=	Year 3 Cash Flow

Net Present Value	Internal Rate of Return	Payback Period

Constraint Summary

Throughput Impact
Operating Expenses Impact
ROI Impact

Approvals

All proposals	Financial analyst signature	Attorney signature
< $25,000	Department manager signature	
$25,000+	CEO signature	

The "Project Type" selected on the form dictates the type of analysis that will be applied to the proposal. A constraint improvement will be examined based on the impact of the proposal on company throughput, cost reductions, and/or return on investment. Discounted cash flow analysis can be applied to cost reduction investments, while several of the other project types indicate that the company is required to make an investment, irrespective of the level of return (if any) on the investment.

Capital Expenditure Proposal Analysis

Reviewing a capital expenditure proposal does not necessarily mean passing judgment on it exactly as presented. A variety of modifications can be made to a proposal, which may result in a more precisely targeted investment or no investment at all. Here are some examples:

- *Asset capacity*. Does the asset have more capacity than is actually needed under the circumstances? Is there a history of usage spikes that call for extra capacity? Depending on the answers to these questions, consider using smaller assets with less capacity. If the asset is powered, this may also lead to reductions in utility costs, installation costs, and floor space requirements.
- *Asset commoditization*. Wherever possible, avoid custom-designed machinery in favor of standard models that are readily available. By doing so, it is easier to obtain repair parts, and there may even be an aftermarket for disposing of the asset when the company no longer needs it.
- *Asset features*. Managers have a habit of wanting to buy new assets with all of the latest features. Are all of these features really needed? If an asset is being replaced, then it is useful to compare the characteristics of the old and new assets, and examine any differences between the two to see if they are required. If the asset is the only model offered by the supplier, would the supplier be willing to strip away some features and offer it at a lower price?
- *Asset standardization*. If a company needs a particular asset in large quantities, then adopt a policy of always buying from the same manufacturer, and preferably only buying the same asset every time. By doing so, the maintenance staff becomes extremely familiar with the maintenance requirements of several identical machines, and only has to stock replacement parts for one model.
- *Expenditure reduction*. A capital proposal likely includes a projection of reduced costs. Verify that these costs are of a sufficiently incremental nature that the cash flows will actually be realized. For example, eliminating 10% of the workload of a salaried employee does not reduce any cost.
- *Extended useful life*. A manager may be applying for an asset replacement simply because the original asset has reached the end of its recommended useful life. But is it really necessary to replace the asset? Consider conducting a formal review of these assets to see if they can still be used for some additional period of time. There may be additional maintenance costs involved, but this will almost certainly be lower than the cost of replacing the asset. However, a concern is that the old asset may be significantly less efficient than its proposed replacement.
- *Facility analysis*. If a capital proposal involves the acquisition of additional facility space, consider reviewing any existing space to see if it can be

compressed, thereby eliminating the need for more space. For example, shift storage items to less expensive warehouse space, shift from offices to more space-efficient cubicles, and encourage employees to work from home or on a later shift. If none of these ideas work, then at least consider acquiring new facilities through a sublease, which tends to require shorter lease terms than a lease arranged with the primary landlord.

- *Monument elimination.* A company may have a large fixed asset around which the rest of the production area is configured; this is called a monument. If there is a monument, consider adopting a policy of using a larger number of lower-capacity assets. By doing so, one can avoid the risk of having a single monument asset go out of service and stopping all production, in favor of having multiple units among which work can be shifted if one unit fails.

The sponsors of capital proposals frequently do *not* appreciate this additional review of their proposals, since it implies that they did not consider these issues themselves. Nonetheless, the savings can be substantial, and so are well worth the aggravation of dealing with annoyed managers.

If the additional review indicates some promising alternatives that may substantially reduce the cost of a proposal, if not eliminate it entirely, then it may be politically wise to route the proposed changes through the controller or chief financial officer, who may have the clout to force a serious review of the alternatives by the project sponsor.

Capital Budgeting Problems

There are several issues with capital budgeting, some of which are caused by the volume and complexity of investment proposals received, and others by the nature of the budgeting process. Two issues arising from large numbers of proposals are:

- *Project interdependencies.* It may be necessary to review how different investment proposals interact with each other. For example, if a proposal to double the capacity of a paint booth is rejected, does this make the investment in a downstream drying room superfluous? Consequently, it may be necessary to first determine the interdependencies of groups of investment proposals, calculate the return on investment for each group, and then decide whether all of the proposals should be accepted.
- *Conflicting projects.* In some organizations, investment proposals are arriving from many departments, without anyone having first reviewed them to see if any of the proposals conflict with each other. For example, one proposal might be to renovate a production line while another proposal is to outsource all production to a third party.

These two issues call for a substantial amount of review time by an analyst who acts as a central coordinator of the capital budgeting process. Two other problems that persistently arise in many budgeting systems are:

- *Corporate bank concept.* The traditional budgeting system has an especially pernicious impact on capital budgeting. The problem is that the budgeting timeline forces most capital budgeting requests to be submitted within a short time period each year, after which additional funds are only grudgingly issued. In effect, this means that the corporate "bank" is only open for business for a month or two every year. Thus, someone may spot an excellent business opportunity for the company, but not be able to take advantage of it for many months, when the "bank" is again open for business. This can be a massive impediment to the continuing growth of a business.
- *Funding incentive.* Given the "bank" issue just noted, managers fight hard for the maximum amount of funding as soon as the "bank" opens – and they spend *all* of it. But when was the last time that you saw a manager return allocated funds, because he did not feel that the expenditure was needed any longer? That is indeed a rare event! Instead, many managers receive their annual allocation of capital expenditure funds and then push for *more* funds throughout the budget year for additional projects. In short, the capital budgeting process really creates a *minimum* funding level, above which a company is very likely to go as the year progresses. It is a rare company that only spends what it initially budgets for fixed assets.

In summary, the budgeting process itself creates two capital budgeting problems. First, it is unusually difficult to obtain funds outside of the budget period, even for deserving projects. And second, managers tend to game the system, so that the capital budgeting process nearly always ends up absorbing more funds than senior management originally intended.

Opportunity Costs

An investment proposal may involve the use of corporate resources that are not stated in the proposal in monetary terms. For example, the purchase of a machine with unusually tight tolerances might require the ongoing time of the industrial engineering staff to monitor it. Or, an investment can call for the permanent use of a large amount of square footage in the production area that will keep this space from being used for other activities. The cost of using these corporate resources is known as opportunity cost, which is defined as the profit lost when one alternative is selected over another.

When there is a situation in which an opportunity cost appears to be present, evaluate the profit that could otherwise be generated if an investment proposal is rejected. For example, if the previously-noted machine with tight tolerances were to be avoided, the industrial engineering staff could spend more time setting up additional production jobs, from which additional profits can be generated.

EXAMPLE

The owner of a manufacturing company located in Colorado is contemplating the purchase of equipment that will expand the company's ability to produce widgets on short notice. However, the legalization of marijuana within the state also means that the owner could easily sublease to a cannabis grower the facility space that would otherwise be taken up by the new equipment. The estimated amount of this sublease is $10,000 per month, which is the opportunity cost of the investment decision.

An area in which to be cautious about the opportunity cost concept is management time. The efforts of the management team related to an investment decision will certainly spike as part of an installation. However, this time investment tends to flatten out quickly, once the company becomes familiar with the operational characteristics of an acquired asset.

Sunk Costs

A sunk cost is a cost that an entity has incurred, and which it can no longer recover by any means. Sunk costs should not be considered when making the decision to continue investing in an ongoing project, since it is not possible to recover the cost. However, many managers continue investing in projects because of the sheer size of the amounts already invested in the past. They do not want to "lose the investment" by curtailing a project that is proving to not be profitable, so they continue pouring more cash into it. Rationally, they should consider earlier investments to be sunk costs, and therefore exclude them from consideration when deciding whether to continue with further investments.

An accounting issue that encourages this adverse behavior is that capitalized costs associated with a project must be written off to expense as soon as the decision is made to cancel the project. When the amount to be written off is quite large, this encourages managers to keep projects running.

Here are several examples of sunk costs:

- *Marketing study.* A company spends $50,000 on a marketing study to see if its new auburn widget will succeed in the marketplace. The study concludes that the widget will not be profitable. At this point, the $50,000 is a sunk cost. The company should not continue with further investments in the widget project, despite the size of the earlier investment.
- *Research and development.* A company invests $2,000,000 over several years to develop a left-handed smoke shifter. Once created, the market is indifferent, and buys no units. The $2,000,000 development cost is a sunk cost, and so should not be considered in any decision to continue or terminate the product.
- *Training.* A company spends $20,000 to train its sales staff in the use of new tablet computers, which they will use to take customer orders. The computers

prove to be unreliable, and the sales manager wants to discontinue their use. The training is a sunk cost, and so should not be considered in any decision regarding the computers.

Excessive Optimism

A central problem to be aware of when examining an investment proposal is the almost inevitable presence of overly optimistic projections. Managers want their proposals to be approved, and so tend to incorporate excessively high revenue estimates and low expense estimates, with predictably massive profit and cash flow projections. Optimism can also lead the sponsor to downgrade the negative effects of outside influences, such as price competition from market entrants, the effects of raw materials shortages, the pricing demands of powerful distribution channels, and so forth.

What if a project sponsor is correct and a project turns out to be wildly profitable? A likely outcome is that the success of the project attracts competitors, who drive down prices. There may be a delay before competitors appear (especially if there are barriers to market entry), but they *will* appear, at which point profits can be expected to tumble.

When analyzing investment proposals, verify that all possible negative effects have been addressed. In addition, if a project sponsor has a habit of presenting excessive benefits, create an alternative set of numbers that are based on more reasonable projections, and see if the outcome is still worthy of an investment. Comparing the outcome of this alternative investment analysis to the one originally proposed can prove to be quite illuminating, especially in regard to how drastically the proposal was originally skewed in a favorable direction.

Capital Rationing

The typical organization only has a limited pool of funds available at any time for investments in fixed assets. The amount available is constrained by its ability to raise additional funds from a combination of borrowings and the sale of stock. The ability to raise funds may be tightly restricted for a number of reasons, such as:

- *Lending crisis*. There are periodic crises in the banking system, when lenders are more interested in calling existing loans than in extending new ones. In this environment, borrowed cash is essentially not available.
- *Historical results*. Even in a loose money environment, lenders may have no interest in lending money when a company has a history of inadequate financial results, since the risk of default is high.
- *Market feedback*. A company's entire industry may have fallen into disfavor with the investment community, so that the sale of stock can only be achieved at low multiples of sales or profits, which may significantly reduce the ownership percentages of existing shareholders.
- *Privately held*. A company may be owned by a small number of investors who are not interested in expanding the ownership to a new group of investors, which effectively cuts off equity as a source of funding.

Alternatively, there may be adequate funding, but the management team does not believe it has sufficient time to oversee more than a certain number of projects. Or, the owners of a business believe in maintaining a conservative debt level, and so will not take on additional debt, irrespective of the presence of tempting investment projects.

In these cases, management may have more qualified investment proposals than it can fund. If so, it must impose capital rationing, where it uses a special set of criteria to decide which proposals to accept. There are a number of ways in which to deal with this situation, which are:

- *Support strategic direction.* If management wants to re-orient the company in a specific direction, it can invest the bulk of available funds in this area, irrespective of the net present value or internal rate of return indicated for individual investment proposals. This places a focus on long-term outcomes, but tends to ignore high-return short-term projects.
- *Use highest outcomes.* If discounted cash flow analysis is being used, select those proposals having the highest net present value or internal rate of return. This approach results in "cherry picking" a selection of projects that yield the best return on investment, but which may not be coordinated from a strategic perspective. The discount rate can be increased in order to determine which investment proposals still have a positive net present value.
- *Bottleneck focus.* As noted in the Constraint Analysis chapter, management invests heavily in those parts of the business that support the functioning of the bottleneck operation, and de-emphasize all other investments.

The situation can become more complicated when outlays for certain projects will continue for several years, and capital rationing is ongoing through that period. In this case, an early investment can block later investments from being made because it is absorbing a large part of the available cash.

If management can reasonably predict the absolute amount of cash that will be available for investment in each of the next few years, it can be useful to feed this information back through the organization. Doing so may reorient the managers who usually submit investment proposals, so that they do not waste time creating proposals for marginal investments that will almost certainly not be approved, given the funding constraint.

Capital Budgeting in a Budget Format

The amount and timing of expenditures for fixed assets come from the capital budgeting process, and are easily transferred into a fixed asset table that can be used as a source document for the budgeted balance sheet. Further, it may be useful to include in the schedule a standard amount of capital expenditures for each new employee hired; this typically includes the cost of office furniture and computer equipment. Finally, consider including a reserve in the schedule for as-yet unspecified fixed assets. There will always be unforeseen asset purchases, so be sure to reserve some funds for them.

In addition, a calculation of the depreciation associated with newly-acquired assets can be added to the table. Also include an estimate of the depreciation associated with *existing* assets, which can easily be derived either from the fixed asset tracking spreadsheet or software. This information is used in the budgeted income statement.

The following example illustrates the concepts of scheduling fixed assets and depreciation.

EXAMPLE

Quest Adventure Gear plans to hire 10 administrative staff into one of its divisions during the budget year, and also plans to buy a variety of fixed assets. The following schedule itemizes the major types of fixed assets and the timing of their acquisition. It also includes a summary of the depreciation for both the existing and to-be-acquired assets.

	Quarter 1	Quarter 2	Quarter 3	Quarter 4
Fixed asset purchases:				
Furniture and fixtures	$28,000	$0	$0	$32,000
Office equipment	0	40,000	0	0
Production equipment	100,000	25,000	80,000	0
Vehicles	32,000	0	32,000	0
Unspecified purchases	15,000	15,000	15,000	15,000
Subtotal	$175,000	$80,000	$127,000	$47,000
Purchases for new hires:				
Headcount additions	3	2	1	4
$6,000 × New hires	$18,000	$12,000	$6,000	$24,000
Total fixed asset purchases	$193,000	$92,000	$133,000	$71,000
Depreciation on new purchases:				
Furniture and fixtures (7 year)	$1,000	$1,000	$1,000	$2,142
Office equipment (5 year)	0	2,000	2,000	2,000
Production equipment (10 year)	2,500	3,125	5,125	5,125
Vehicles (5 year)	1,600	1,600	3,200	3,200
Unspecified purchases (5 year)	750	1,500	2,250	3,000
Subtotal	$5,850	$9,225	$13,575	$15,467
Depreciation on existing assets	108,000	107,500	105,000	99,500
Total depreciation	$113,850	$116,725	$118,575	$114,967

It can make sense to develop longer-term capital budgets, such as a five-year budget. This can be useful when there are numerous assets that have determinable useful lives, and which will have to be replaced at known intervals. Such a budget can then be used for long-term planning relating to when funds must be obtained to pay for them.

Capital Budgeting in the Absence of a Budget Model

The process of reviewing and approving capital expenditures can be lengthy and complex. How does this mesh with an environment in which there is no formal budget? Even if there is no budget, there should still be a rolling forecast for expected revenues and expenses over the next few months. Given the presence of a rolling forecast, three prospects for dealing with capital expenditures suggest themselves:

- *Fast track approvals.* Many capital budgeting proposals are positioned at the lower end of the range of possible dollar amounts, and so require both fewer funds and less analysis. For these items, senior management should maintain a pool of funds at all times, and fast track the review process for any capital budget proposals submitted. This process is designed to support the bulk of all capital expenditures needed by front-line teams.
- *Near-term projections.* The treasury staff should maintain a short-term forecast of available cash flow, so that managers can see if cash will be available for capital budget requests. If the forecast indicates a cash flow problem, then projects can be delayed until more funds are available.
- *Long-term projections.* Senior management should maintain a rolling five-year forecast. This can be quite a brief document, showing general estimates of where the market will be, and the company's position within it. Based on this forecast, the company can determine its long-term capital expenditure plans for high-cost items.

Those capital expenditures designated as fast track approvals require no attention from senior management, since the funds involved are not large. However, the largest expenditures should be labeled as strategic commitments, and therefore fall within the responsibility of senior management.

When the annual budget is eliminated, this also means that the annual review of existing projects is eliminated. Instead, it is far better to engage in more frequent reviews of project status. Doing so will reveal problem areas where it makes sense to terminate a project entirely, thereby making more funds available for use in other capital projects. These more frequent reviews should not be excessively detailed, or else they will consume too much time. Instead, have a brief review of the time to completion in comparison to the original estimate, as well as of the funds expended to date in comparison to the original projection. If either of these metrics reveals a significant negative variance, then more analysis is called for.

Capital Budgeting with Minimal Cash

What if a company has very little money to spend on capital investments? If so, the capital budgeting choices may be entirely different. The primary target is to obtain the maximum return on investment as fast as possible, while spending a minimum amount of cash. Here are some options:

- *Repairs*. Evaluate the extent to which the lives of existing equipment can be prolonged, and see if there is old, unused equipment that can be brought back to workable condition with a modest investment in repairs. The cost of these repairs should be limited to a level well below the cost of investing in new equipment. The result may be equipment that is not overly efficient, but this is acceptable as long as the amount of funds invested is low.
- *Operating hours*. See if it is possible to extend the operating hours of the existing equipment. It may be much less expensive to have a few people work overtime or on an additional shift than to buy new equipment. The result could be equipment that runs for all three shifts, though be aware that the cost of maintenance will increase when usage levels go up.
- *Outsource*. It may save cash to outsource work to a third party, even if the cost is higher on a per-unit basis than producing in-house. To keep options open for bringing work back to the company in the future, only sign short-term agreements to outsource work.
- *Buy used equipment*. Place a major emphasis on purchasing used equipment. The market prices of used equipment can be so much less than for new equipment that it may be worthwhile to institute a rule that new equipment can only be acquired with the prior approval of senior management. However, consider the availability of spare parts before acquiring older equipment. If parts are in short supply, it may be inordinately expensive to repair the equipment.
- *Lease assets*. Be sure to institute a lease versus buy analysis (see the Lease or Buy Decision chapter). A lease may carry a relatively high implicit interest rate, but has the particular advantage of deferring the payment of cash to later periods.
- *Cash inflow analysis*. When cash is in short supply, only invest in equipment that will generate an immediate return. This means equipment that can produce verifiable cash flows within a few weeks is much better than equipment that is only intended to provide spare capacity, and which may not be needed immediately. Also, do not acquire equipment for which the associated cash inflows are speculative.

In short, being in survival mode changes the orientation of the capital budgeting process to one where you try to get by with what you have, scrounge for used equipment, and only invest when the offsetting cash inflows are certain. With the orientation on day-to-day survival, there is no long-term analysis of return on investment. Instead, this is a rare case where the much-maligned payback method (as described later in the Other Capital Budgeting Analyses chapter) could be a useful tool, since its focus is on the amount of time required to pay back the initial investment.

There are some issues with the recommendations noted here. First, older equipment is likely to be less efficient, and may require additional maintenance time. Also, the result could be a clutter of equipment that does not work together very well. These points are acceptable in the short term, but should be addressed over the long term, assuming the company has emerged from its cash-poor situation and can afford better equipment.

The Post Installation Review

It is important to conduct a post installation review of any capital expenditure project, to see if the initial expectations for it were realized. If not, then the results of this review can be used to modify the capital budgeting process to include better information in future analyses.

Another reason for having a post installation review is that it provides a control over those managers who fill out the initial capital budgeting proposals. If they know there is no post installation review, then they can wildly overstate the projected results of their projects with impunity, just to have them approved. Of course, this control is only useful if it is conducted relatively soon after a project is completed. Otherwise, the responsible manager may have moved on in his career, and can no longer be tied back to the results of his work.

It is even better to begin a post installation review while a project is still being implemented, and especially when the implementation period is expected to be long. This initial review gives senior management a good idea of whether the cost of a project is staying close to its initial expectations. If not, management may need to authorize more vigorous management of the project, scale it back, or even cancel it outright.

If the post implementation review results in the suspicion that a project proposal was unduly optimistic, this brings up the question of how to deal with the responsible manager. At a minimum, the proposal reviews can flag any future proposals by this reviewer as suspect, and worthy of especially close attention. Another option is to tie long-term compensation to the results of these projects. A third possibility is to include the results of these project reviews in personnel reviews, which may lead to a reduction in employee compensation. A really catastrophic result may even be grounds for the termination of the responsible party.

EXAMPLE

Quest Adventure Gear has just completed a one-year project to increase the amount of production capacity at its primary equipment manufacturing center. The original capital budgeting proposal was for an initial expenditure of $290,000, resulting in additional annual throughput of $100,000 per year. The actual result is somewhat different. The accountant's report includes the following text:

> **Findings:** The proposal only contained the purchase price of the equipment. However, since the machinery was delivered from Germany, Quest also incurred $22,000 of freight charges and $3,000 in customs fees. Further, the project required the installation of a new concrete pad, a breaker box, and electrical wiring that cost an additional $10,000. Finally, the equipment proved to be difficult to configure, and required $20,000 of consulting fees from the manufacturer, as well as $5,000 for the materials scrapped during testing. Thus, the actual cost of the project was $350,000.

Subsequent operation of the equipment reveals that it cannot operate without an average of 20% downtime for maintenance, as opposed to the 5% downtime that was advertised by the manufacturer. This reduces throughput by 15%, which equates to a drop of $15,000 in throughput per year, to $85,000.

Recommendations: To incorporate a more comprehensive set of instructions into the capital budgeting proposal process to account for transportation, setup, and testing costs. Also, given the wide difference between the performance claims of the manufacturer and actual results, to hire a consultant to see if the problem is caused by our installation of the equipment; if not, we recommend not buying from this supplier in the future.

Summary

This chapter gave an overview of the capital budgeting process, and then noted a number of ways to improve upon the initial proposals that may be submitted. These improvements can be distributed throughout the company as standard instructions, so that investment proposals gradually become more refined over time. In addition, we noted a number of issues that can clutter the information in a proposal, such as the presence of sunk costs and overly optimistic projections, which must be constantly guarded against as part of the review process. As a lean alternative to the classic capital budgeting approach, we have also noted how to engage in capital budgeting when there is very little cash available – which can be useful for a startup business that has little initial funding.

Chapter 2
Capital Budgeting Strategy

Introduction

There are many detailed analysis issues to consider when engaged in the capital budgeting process, most of which are covered in the following chapters. In this chapter, we attend to the broader context within which capital budgeting decisions are made. This is the general environment in which the strategic direction of a business is developed. Once the strategy is in place, management can then place boundaries around its capital budgeting process, covering such topics as whether investments will be made at all, and whether there are areas in which the company will withhold or concentrate its funding.

Capacity Expansion Strategy

One of the decisions that can be made is whether to increase the amount of productive capacity of a business. There are several reasons for doing so, which include the following:

- *Increase market share.* If the goods being sold are of the commodity variety (with no differentiating features), then customers are more likely to buy from that supplier offering the lowest prices. If so, it makes sense to invest in the most efficient productive capacity, so that costs can be driven down and prices along with them. There is an expectation that the seller's market share will increase, so the investment must not only involve more efficient operations, but also an expansion of the operations. This can also mean that older production facilities are replaced at regular intervals, so that costs can be driven down as low as possible.
- *Defend market share.* A business may find that the total market size is no longer expanding, and additional competitors are entering the market. If so, it may need to continually upgrade its production capabilities in order to reduce its costs or improve its responsiveness to customer demands. The ability to drive down costs is especially crucial, so that the organization has the flexibility to cut its prices in order to fend off competitors.
- *Increasing market.* In some industries, the total market is continuing to expand. If so, there is a constant struggle to keep up with demand, which calls for ongoing increases in productive capacity. The capacity expansions do not have to involve the most efficient processes, since customers are usually willing to pay higher prices at this stage of the market's life cycle, which allows for higher-cost production.

The preceding discussions about increasing or defending market share all involve predictions of the actions of competitors. The managers of competitors probably all have access to the same market information, but may interpret it differently or are constrained from acting on it, depending on their unique circumstances. For example, one competitor may have gone public, and so is sitting on a large cash reserve, which makes it easier to fund a large capacity increase, even if doing so may result in a low rate of return. Conversely, another competitor may have a long-running practice of outsourcing all production and relying on its design capabilities to create unique products that will command unusually high prices; consequently, it may have no productive capacity to increase. Yet a third business may have recently been bought out by its management team in a leveraged buyout, and has no excess cash to use for asset purchases until it has paid down the debt used to buy out the previous owner. All of these competitor situations must be examined to arrive at estimates of how each one will make capital investment decisions, which in turn could impact the company's own investment decisions.

The outcome of this analysis is a projection of changes in the total productive capacity of the industry. This amount can then be compared to expected customer demand, resulting in an estimate of likely price points through the analysis period. This high-level review can then be used as one of the inputs to a decision to invest in more productive capacity.

EXAMPLE

A common practice in the airline industry is to lease aircraft, rather than buying them directly. Doing so reduces the airlines' financial risk, since they can return airplanes once the underlying leases have expired. An additional benefit is that they can then lease much newer aircraft, thereby refreshing their fleets.

What if there is a new entrant in the market, in the form of a national airline that is funded by an oil-rich state government? This entity can spend inordinate sums to massively increase its passenger capacity, while its backer is willing to absorb large operating losses. In this case, a fundamental part of the capacity analysis is estimating the willingness of the government backer to continue pouring funds into its airline, which in turn is driven by estimates of the price of oil (always a hazardous endeavor).

Capacity Reduction Strategy

A significant strategic decision is to cut back on investments in certain areas. For example, the management team may find that certain product lines are suffering from declining sales and margins. A logical outcome of this analysis is that management cuts off all funding or even begins to dismantle production lines, so that annual capital funding can be reoriented toward areas of the business that are expected to generate better returns.

A capacity reduction strategy is a difficult one to implement, for those employees working in the areas targeted for reduction have a vested interest in continuing investments, and so will lobby hard to take their traditional share of the total pool of investments. Further, every aspect of a business is designed to support its existing direction, so there is a strong tendency to support the current thrust of operations (the momentum principle). Consequently, a capacity reduction tends to occur later than it should, possibly at the point when further investments really should have been curtailed several years earlier.

Growth Strategy

Investors may have given a company a strong mandate to grow sales as rapidly as possible. This is most common in a startup environment, where a venture capital backer wants to turbocharge sales in order to massively increase the valuation of the investee. A growth strategy may also be fueled by the funds received when a company goes public, where investors are willing to buy shares in exchange for the prospect of strong sales growth that will increase the value of their shares. A growth strategy may also be possible when a firm has access to funds at a very low cost, perhaps through a bond issuance at a low interest rate, and so has *a lot* of money available for capital investments. In these situations, the need for growth alters some aspects of the capital budgeting process, especially in the following areas:

- *Project selection.* Management is more willing to invest in a broad range of projects, to assist in finding those few opportunities that will trigger unusually strong sales growth. There is a tendency to invest in entirely new projects, rather than enhancing existing operations.
- *Risk appetite.* The firm is more willing to lose money on unusually risky projects, as long as there is a possibility of outsized sales growth.
- *Hurdle rate.* The firm adopts a low hurdle rate, so that most projects will receive some consideration, rather than being automatically rejected if they do not provide an adequate return on investment.
- *Process formality.* The firm is more willing to invest money in a less structured process, such as paying out funds with little review when the amounts involved are small.
- *Process focus.* A firm may find that it should be investing funds in reimagining its processes to make them more productive and to support customers better, in addition to investing the funds in fixed assets.

In general, the mindset in a growth environment is to treat capital investments as experiments; some will inevitably fail, but that is the price to be paid for finding a few gold nuggets in the mix of investments. This mindset also means that the business is willing to shed those projects that do not appear to have good prospects for success.

Risk Levels

Additions to or upgrades of a company's productive capacity may require substantial design and construction work, which could drive the completion date well into the future. If so, a significant risk is being imposed on management, that it can reliably project market conditions not only as of the start date of the new productive capacity, but also during its entire useful life – which could extend for several decades into the future. The risk level associated with a long-duration investment differs greatly, depending on the environment. Here are several considerations, presented in increasing order of risk:

- *Equipment replacement.* The least-risky investment is one in which existing equipment is being replaced. In this situation, management already knows what the demand is for its products, and only seeks to replace the mode of production by which that demand level is fulfilled. There are two variations on this concept, each with different risk levels. They are:

  - o *Large number of small customers.* When there are many customers and none of them comprise a large proportion of sales, this is an ideal situation for the organization, for it is not subject to the purchasing whims of a few large customers. An equipment replacement in this environment can be considered relatively safe.
  - o *Most sales to a few large customers.* When the bulk of all sales are being made to a small number of large customers, the organization is at risk of losing a significant part of its sales if just one or two customers decide to take their business elsewhere.

- *Same market, product line extension.* When a product is being added to an existing product line and is filling an obvious hole in the lineup, expending funds for related production equipment tends to be a lower-risk activity. There is already an established market and there is presumably an active marketing campaign supporting the entire product line, so there is a reasonable expectation that sales will be generated.
- *Same market, capacity exceeds existing requirements.* When management wants to increase market share, it is essentially investing in production capacity for which there is currently no demand. This can be quite risky, especially when competitors are expected to defend their market share with price cuts.
- *Different market, no knowledge of demand.* A highly risky endeavor is to invest in fixed assets to support an entirely new product in a new market for which the organization has no selling experience. There is a risk that demand will be low or zero, in which case the capital investment will be a loss.

A particular problem is when a number of companies all invest in new capacity, possibly because they expect an overall increase in the size of the market – which does not appear. When this happens, the fixed cost of the industry is now higher, for which the usual solution is price-cutting by everyone in the industry, in order to fill their capacity. This situation may persist for years, as companies prefer to maintain their higher capacity levels and hope that some other competitor will shut down their facilities or go bankrupt.

An additional risk issue is the time required to add capacity. When the time period required is relatively short, management can use current demand levels and short-term projections as the basis for an investment decision, which is relatively low risk. This situation is most common when the lead time to have fixed assets manufactured is low, as is the time required to install the assets, test them, and have them ready for production. Conversely, the construction of a major new facility may take years, which increases the risk that demand levels will shift downward before the facility is ready for use.

> **Tip:** To ensure that risk is addressed, involve the company's risk manager in all capital expenditure decisions above a certain threshold level. The risk manager can point out potential problems and suggest changes to mitigate risk.

Additional Risk Factors for International Investments

There are additional risk factors to ponder when a foreign investment is being contemplated. The following points should be considered:

- *Cash repatriation.* Some governments lock down or severely restrict the ability of companies to shift cash earned within their borders to locations elsewhere in the world. Or, cash transfers may be allowed but only after a stiff transfer tax has been paid. If so, this cash is only available for investment within the borders of that country.
- *Asset expropriation.* Is there a history or threat of asset expropriation by the government? If so, does it make sense to own assets within the country, or would it be more prudent to lease assets or outsource asset-intensive operations? This issue can be modeled by developing an investment model where cash flows terminate abruptly as of the date when an expropriation can be expected.
- *Transfer pricing disputes.* The local tax authorities may take issue with the prices that the parent company assigns to its own sub-assemblies and raw materials being sold to the local operation for further transformative activities. If so, the parent may be forced to alter its prices, thereby shifting taxable income into higher-tax jurisdictions. The result can be a lower after-tax profit from an investment.
- *Local monetary policy.* A few countries print far more money than they should, or routinely default on their international borrowings. Because of these practices, the currencies of these countries tend to suffer from periodic and sharp downward adjustments in their exchange rates, reducing their value. Investing in this environment can be highly risky, since even profitable operations will spin off cash that is rapidly declining in value.
- *Cost of hedging alternatives.* There may be ways to mitigate the effects of currency exchange anomalies by using different types of hedges (see the author's *Corporate Cash Management* course). However, when there is a history of substantial swings in the exchange rate, the cost of hedging can be uneconomical. One should be aware of this hedging cost before committing to an investment.

A company may still choose to invest in an environment where the preceding factors clearly point toward a high level of risk. Such a decision may still make sense, if the long-term benefit is perceived to be good. This may be particularly the case when a company wants to secure a competitive advantage by exploring a market and building its brand with consumers before any of the more hesitant competitors are willing to dabble in the market. Nonetheless, investing in a country with numerous risk indicators can be a dangerous proposition.

Factors Impacting Future Asset Usage

Besides the market share issues noted in the preceding sections, the capital budgeting strategy decision must also incorporate a number of additional factors, all of which can have a profound impact on the profitability of an investment decision.

A major concern is the direction of technological enhancements to the assets used by a business. If there has been a continuing pattern of ongoing enhancements, it is possible that the company will be forced to continually upgrade its equipment, so that the useful life of each asset may be quite short. This can have the effect of forcing management to only invest in assets that have a high probability of return on investment, since they must achieve payback in short order. However, it may also mean that a robust secondary market has developed for used assets, so that assets can be sold off and replaced without an overly negative financial impact.

Another issue is the cost of raw materials. If supplies are constrained, this will increase the cost of the resulting product, which in turn will likely trigger a price increase. If so, and there are obvious substitutes available, one can reasonably expect demand to decline, which can result in a large amount of underutilized assets. This factor is more likely to arise when raw material sources are located in areas of the world that are subject to natural disasters, or which have unstable political situations.

Yet another concern is the actions of competitors. Unless an industry is unusually staid, it is likely that at least a few competitors will attempt to make aggressive moves to expand their profitability, which may come at the expense of the other industry participants. For example, there may be initiatives to cut prices, guarantee faster delivery, add more features, increase the length of product warranties, add distribution centers, provide free training, and so forth – all of which alter the competitive environment.

EXAMPLE

The management of Ambivalence Corporation is about to make a large investment in its potion brewing production facility that will allow it to reduce costs significantly and thereby offer lower prices to its customers. The team learns that a major competitor has decided to construct warehouses in several key customer locations, so that it can offer same-day delivery to customers in these areas. The strategic direction of the competitor is therefore focused on higher service, rather than lower prices.

Should Ambivalence match this competitor move by constructing its own distribution network, or continue with its low-cost, low-price strategy?

Another concern is possibly constrained cash flows. This means that a business may be able to generate positive cash flows, but is unable to use them. For example, the tax department may advocate shifting funds offshore, where income is taxed at a lower rate. However, doing so may make it difficult to repatriate the funds in order to invest in fixed assets. Similarly (and as already noted), an entity may have highly profitable operations in a country that imposes strict cash controls, so that funds cannot be shifted out of the country. In this case as well, internal cash may not be available, so that the company is limited in its investment decisions by its ability to raise debt or equity funding from outside sources.

Another concern appears in industries where the primary competitive focus is only selling at the lowest price (common in commodity environments). In this case, it is possible that the size of facilities gradually increase in order to achieve higher and higher levels of scale, so that unit costs decline. In this situation, each successive generation of production facilities is larger than the one before it, which introduces ever-larger production capacity into the market. The likely outcome is an excessive amount of capacity in relation to demand, so that prices are depressed for a long period of time. In this situation, a management team is faced with the decision to either put a large amount of cash at risk of not generating a sufficient return, or of not investing at all and exiting the market. Neither choice is an enticing one.

Perceived Certainty of Future Demand

The amount of investment that businesses are willing to put into new fixed assets is dependent to a significant extent on the certainty of demand. If there is a history of steady increases in customer demand, with little variation, then competitors tend to make continual investments in assets. In this situation, a common investment strategy is to try to bring capacity on line faster than competitors, and to use public announcements to signal this intent. The intent behind this strategy is to force other companies to back down from their own investment plans, leaving the most aggressive firms to gain market share.

The situation differs when there is much uncertainty regarding the amount of future customer demand. Perhaps there has been a history of irregular sales levels, or perhaps changes in technology make future demand unusually difficult to predict. Or, there is a history of cyclical demand, but the peaks and valleys in the cycles are difficult to predict. In these situations, the more aggressive firms are more likely to make substantial investments, though this places them at risk of incurring major losses if customer demand does not materialize within a reasonable period of time. Conversely, those firms whose managers harbor doubts about future demand growth are more likely to wait for actual demand figures to settle down before committing to significant capital investments.

Duration

There may be instances in which there are multiple possible investment choices, but the durations of the investments are different. For example, one investment generates a 20% return, but only for a single year, while another generates an 18% return for the next five years. There is a strategic issue here, which is management's expectation for the direction of future interest rates. If there is an expectation of increasing interest rates, this means that the company's cost of capital will increase over time, which makes it more difficult to generate a return. In this environment, it makes more sense to invest in short-duration investments, so that they can be replaced by higher-return investments in the future. Conversely, an expectation of lower interest rates in the future would lead management to seek out longer-duration investments.

The concept of duration is most important in a highly inflationary environment, where it can make sense to only engage in the briefest investments, perhaps with a preference to outsource work to third parties so that they incur the risk of below-grade returns on *their* investments.

Impact of Financing Alternatives

When credit is tight, companies must be exceedingly prudent in making capital budgeting choices. But what about when the reverse situation arises? Lenders may periodically have abundant cash available, and may even lower their lending requirements in order to put this cash to work. Suppliers may also offer easy credit, especially when doing so is perceived to be a competitive advantage against their fellow suppliers. In this environment, the management team could certainly relax its evaluation criteria for making capital investments, possibly resulting in some investments not yielding an adequate return. However, the situation is somewhat more complex, as the following points will impact the investment decision:

- *Ease with which assets are returned.* A company may be more inclined to make investments when suppliers are willing to accept the assets back on short notice. This is a rare situation, but can occur when suppliers are under intense pressure to make sales. In this case, the risk of failure is essentially being shifted back to suppliers.
- *Collateral restrictions.* A company is more likely to take advantage of a low-cost financing offer when the effect of a failure on the rest of the business is minimized. For example, when the lender has no rights to attach any assets other than the purchased asset in the event of a payment default, the management team has limited its losses, and so is more likely to invest in an asset.
- *Personal liability.* In a smaller business, the owner may have to personally guarantee payment on a loan, in which case all investment decisions are likely to be highly prudent, no matter how low the cost of funds may be. This is not the case for professional managers in a larger entity, where lenders do not impose personal guarantees on the management team.

Summary

When reading about the use of capital budgeting analysis techniques in the following chapters, keep in mind that the numbers under review are based on one or more management judgments regarding probable future scenarios. These judgments could prove to be wildly incorrect, which brings into question the extent to which any analysis method is used to derive fine distinctions between different investment proposals. The only time when investment decisions can be viewed from an accurate perspective is in hindsight – analyses that are based on projections are bound to be wrong to some extent. Nonetheless, this does not mean that capital budgeting should be abandoned – far from it. Instead, one must understand which elements of an analysis are based on firm data that is unlikely to change, and which parts are based on estimates of market conditions that are outside of the control of the company.

Chapter 3
Discounted Cash Flow Analysis

Introduction

One of the most accepted methods for making a capital budgeting decision is to focus on the cash inflows and outflows associated with an investment. If the net amount of these cash flows (adjusted for the time value of money) is positive, then a proposed investment is accepted.

When evaluating investments, it is critical to understand the time value of money, and how it relates to the analysis of cash flows. In this chapter, we address the time value of money concept and describe present and future value tables, followed by descriptions of two discounted cash flow techniques – net present value and the internal rate of return. We also make note of terminal value and the types of information that should be included in a cash flow analysis.

> **Related Podcast Episode:** Episode 147 of the Accounting Best Practices Podcast discusses net present value analysis. It is available at: **accountingtools.com/podcasts** or **iTunes**

Cash Flows

What are cash flows? These are the increases or decreases in the cash balance experienced by an entity as the result of a specific investment. For example, buying a machine results in a negative cash flow as of the point in time when the supplier is paid. Thus, a negative cash flow might be delayed if the buyer can obtain delayed payment terms or can make payments in a series of installments. Similarly, cash inflows occur when an organization experiences an increase in its cash account. The following example expands upon the concept.

EXAMPLE

Hammer Industries invests in a stamping machine, which costs $50,000. The supplier sends an invoice on March 1, to be paid on April 1. Hammer pays the invoice on April 1, so a negative cash flow occurs on that date – not on March 1, when the invoice was received.

Hammer's industrial engineering staff spends one month installing and testing the stamping machine. The company then uses the machine to produce a batch of widgets, which it sells to a customer on May 10, with net 30 day terms. The customer pays on time, resulting in positive cash flows on June 9 – not on May 10, when the invoice was issued.

The cash flow concept is used throughout this chapter.

Time Value of Money

The foundation of discounted cash flow analysis is the concept that cash received to-day is more valuable than cash received at some point in the future. The reason is that someone who agrees to receive payment at a later date foregoes the ability to invest that cash right now. The only way for someone to agree to a delayed payment is to pay them for the privilege, which is known as interest income.

For example, if a person owns $10,000 now and invests it at an interest rate of 10%, then she will have earned $1,000 by having use of the money for one year. If she were instead to *not* have access to that cash for one year, then she would lose the $1,000 of interest income. The interest income in this example represents the time value of money.

To extend the example, what is the current payout of cash at which the person would be indifferent to receiving cash now or in one year? In essence, what is the amount that, when invested at 10%, will equal $10,000 in one year? The general formula used to answer this question, known as the *present value of 1 due in N periods*, is:

$$\frac{1}{(1 + \text{Interest rate})^{\text{Number of years}}}$$

The calculation for the example is:

$$\frac{\$10,000}{(1 + 10\%)^{1 \text{ year}}}$$

$$= \$9,090.91$$

In essence, if the person receives $9,090.91 now and invests it at a 10% interest rate, her cash balance will have increased to $10,000 in one year.

The effect of the present value formula becomes more pronounced if the receipt of cash is delayed to a date even further in the future, because the period during which the recipient of the cash cannot invest the cash is prolonged.

The concept of the time value of money also works in reverse, for expenditures. There is a monetary value associated with delaying the payment of cash, which is known as the *future amount of 1 due in N periods*. The general formula used to address this situation is:

$$\text{Amount deferred} \times (1 + \text{Interest rate})^{\text{Number of years}}$$

For example, if a person could delay the expenditure of $10,000 for one year and could invest the funds during that year at a 10% interest rate, the value of the deferred expenditure would be $11,000 in one year.

One of the common uses of the time value of money is to derive the present value of an annuity. An annuity is a series of payments that occur in the same amounts and at the same intervals over a period of time. An annuity is a common feature of a capital budgeting analysis, where a consistent stream of cash flows is expected for multiple years if a fixed asset is purchased. For example, a company is contemplating the purchase of a production line for $3,000,000, which will generate net positive cash flows of $1,000,000 per year for the next five years. This stream of incoming cash flows is an annuity. The formula used to derive the present value of an *ordinary annuity of 1 per period* is:

$$1 - \frac{1}{(1 + \text{Interest rate})^{\text{Number of years}}}$$
$$\overline{\text{Interest rate}}$$

The preceding formula is for an *ordinary annuity*, which is an annuity where payments are made at the end of each period. If cash were instead received at the beginning of each period, the annuity would be called an *annuity due*, and would be formulated somewhat differently.

Present and Future Value Tables

In the last section, we discussed the general concept of the time value of money, and how this value can be translated into the present value formula. The concept is most commonly employed in an electronic spreadsheet. For example, the present value formula in Excel is:

$$(1/(1+\text{Interest rate})^{\wedge}\text{Number of years})$$

As an example, if the discount rate is 10% and you want to determine the discount for cash flows that will occur three years in the future, the Excel calculation is:

$$(1/(1+0.1)^{\wedge}3) = 0.75131$$

The easiest way to calculate present value is to use the preceding formula in Excel for the monetary amount and time period in question. However, what if an electronic spreadsheet is not available? The present value discount factor can also be derived from a present value table, which is commonly available in textbooks and on the Internet. The following present value table states the discount factors for the present value of 1 due in N periods for a common range of interest rates.

Present Value Factors for 1 Due in N Periods

Number of Years	6%	7%	8%	9%	10%	11%	12%
1	0.9434	0.9346	0.9259	0.9174	0.9091	0.9009	0.8929
2	0.8900	0.8734	0.8573	0.8417	0.8265	0.8116	0.7972
3	0.8396	0.8163	0.7938	0.7722	0.7513	0.7312	0.7118
4	0.7921	0.7629	0.7350	0.7084	0.6830	0.6587	0.6355
5	0.7473	0.7130	0.6806	0.6499	0.6209	0.5935	0.5674
6	0.7050	0.6663	0.6302	0.5963	0.5645	0.5346	0.5066
7	0.6651	0.6228	0.5835	0.5470	0.5132	0.4817	0.4524
8	0.6274	0.5820	0.5403	0.5019	0.4665	0.4339	0.4039
9	0.5919	0.5439	0.5003	0.4604	0.4241	0.3909	0.3606
10	0.5584	0.5084	0.4632	0.4224	0.3855	0.3522	0.3220
11	0.5268	0.4751	0.4289	0.3875	0.3505	0.3173	0.2875
12	0.4970	0.4440	0.3971	0.3555	0.3186	0.2858	0.2567
13	0.4688	0.4150	0.3677	0.3262	0.2897	0.2575	0.2292
14	0.4423	0.3878	0.3405	0.2993	0.2633	0.2320	0.2046
15	0.4173	0.3625	0.3152	0.2745	0.2394	0.2090	0.1827

To use the table, move to the column representing the relevant interest rate, and move down to the "number of years" row indicating the discount rate to apply to the applicable year of cash flow. Thus, if an analysis were to indicate $100,000 of cash flow in the fourth year, and the interest rate were 10%, multiply the $100,000 by 0.6830 to arrive at a present value of $68,300 for those cash flows.

The same table format is also available for determining the present value of an ordinary annuity of 1 per period. This table is used to derive the present value of a series of annuity payments. The multipliers for this calculation are noted in the following table.

Present Value Factors for Ordinary Annuity of 1 per Period

Number of Years	6%	7%	8%	9%	10%	11%	12%
1	0.9434	0.9346	0.9259	0.9174	0.9091	0.9009	0.8929
2	1.8334	1.8080	1.7833	1.7591	1.7355	1.7125	1.6901
3	2.6730	2.6243	2.5771	2.5313	2.4869	2.4437	2.4018
4	3.4651	3.3872	3.3121	3.2397	3.1699	3.1024	3.0373
5	4.2124	4.1002	3.9927	3.8897	3.7908	3.6959	3.6048
6	4.9173	4.7665	4.6229	4.4859	4.3553	4.2305	4.1114
7	5.5824	5.3893	5.2064	5.0330	4.8684	4.7122	4.5638
8	6.2098	5.9713	5.7466	5.5348	5.3349	5.1461	4.9676
9	6.8017	6.5152	6.2469	5.9952	5.7590	5.5370	5.3282
10	7.3601	7.0236	6.7101	6.4177	6.1446	5.8892	5.6502
11	7.8869	7.4987	7.1390	6.8052	6.4951	6.2065	5.9377
12	8.3838	7.9427	7.5361	7.1607	6.8137	6.4924	6.1944
13	8.8527	8.3577	7.9038	7.4869	7.1034	6.7499	6.4235
14	9.2950	8.7455	8.2442	7.7862	7.3667	6.9819	6.6282
15	9.7122	9.1079	8.5595	8.0607	7.6061	7.1909	6.8109

The annuity table contains a multiplier specific to the number of payments over which you expect to receive a series of equal payments and at a certain discount rate. When this factor is multiplied by one of the payments, it yields the present value of the stream of payments. For example, if you expect to receive five payments of $10,000 each and use a discount rate of 8%, then the factor would be 3.9927 (as noted in the preceding table in the intersection of the 8% column and the row for five years). Then multiply the 3.9927 factor by $10,000 to arrive at a present value of the annuity of $39,927.

Net Present Value

Net present value (NPV) analysis is useful for determining the current value of a stream of cash flows that extend out into the future. NPV is commonly used in the analysis of capital purchasing requests, to see if an initial payment for fixed assets and other expenditures will generate net positive cash flows. In essence, if the outcome is positive, then invest in the project. If not, then avoid the investment.

NPV can also be used to compare the expected cash flows for different projects, to decide which has the largest present value and is therefore more worthy of an investment.

To calculate net present value, we use the following formula:

$$NPV = X \times [(1+r)^n - 1]/[r \times (1+r)^n]$$

Where:

> X = The amount received per period
> n = The number of periods
> r = The rate of return

It is not that difficult to estimate the amount of cash received per period, as well as the number of periods over which cash will be received. The difficult inclusion in the formula is the rate of return. This is generally considered to be a company's average cost of capital, but can also be considered its incremental cost of capital, or a risk-adjusted cost of capital. In the latter case, this means that several extra percentage points are added to the corporate cost of capital for those cash flow situations considered to be unusually risky. The cost of capital is discussed in the next chapter.

EXAMPLE

The CFO of Franklin Drilling is interested in the NPV associated with a production facility that the CEO wants to acquire. In exchange for an initial $10 million payment, Franklin should receive payments of $1.2 million at the end of each of the next 15 years. Franklin has a corporate cost of capital of 9%. To calculate the NPV, we insert the cash flow information into the NPV formula:

$$1,200,000 \times ((1+0.09)^{15}-1)/(0.09 \times (1+0.09)^{15}) = \$9,672,826$$

The present value of the cash flows associated with the investment is $327,174 lower than the initial investment in the facility, so Franklin should not proceed with the investment.

EXAMPLE

Milagro Corporation is planning to acquire an asset that it expects will yield positive cash flows for the next five years. Its cost of capital is 10%, which it uses as the discount rate to construct the net present value of the project. The following table shows the calculation:

Year	Cash Flow	10% Discount Factor	Present Value
0	-$500,000	1.0000	-$500,000
1	+130,000	0.9091	+118,183
2	+130,000	0.8265	+107,445
3	+130,000	0.7513	+97,669
4	+130,000	0.6830	+88,790
5	+130,000	0.6209	+80,717
		Net Present Value	-$7,196

The net present value of the proposed project is negative at the 10% discount rate, so Milagro should not invest in it.

A net present value calculation that truly reflects the reality of cash flows will likely be more complex than the one shown in the preceding example. It is best to break down the analysis into a number of sub-categories, to see exactly when cash flows are occurring and with what activities they are associated. Here are the more common contents of a net present value analysis:

- *Asset purchases.* All of the expenditures associated with the purchase, delivery, installation, and testing of the asset being purchased.
- *Asset-linked expenses.* Any ongoing expenses, such as warranty agreements, property taxes, and maintenance, that are associated with the asset.
- *Asset retirement obligations.* In some instances, the local government may require that a facility be dismantled and environmental remediation efforts completed at the end of the useful life of a project. For example, the retirement of a nuclear power plant can require years of effort and a substantial expenditure.
- *Cash from sale of asset.* If an asset is to be purchased, also assume that some cash will be received at a later date from the eventual sale of that asset.
- *Contribution margin.* Any incremental cash flows resulting from sales that can be attributed to a project.
- *Depreciation effect.* Each fixed asset will be depreciated, and this depreciation shelters a portion of any net income from income taxes, so note the income tax reduction caused by depreciation. Depreciation is a noncash charge, since it only reduces the amount of an existing asset; there is no cash outflow associated with depreciation. For example, if $100 of depreciation can be deducted from taxable income and the tax rate is 35%, there is a $35 positive cash flow effect associated with the depreciation expense. For this analysis, the tax depreciation associated with an asset should be used, in case there is a difference between the tax depreciation and book depreciation.
- *Expense reductions.* Any incremental expense reductions caused by the project, such as automation that eliminates direct labor hours.
- *Maintenance costs.* If there will be incremental costs incurred to maintain a purchased asset, include the cash flows associated with these costs. Do not include any cash flows related to maintenance personnel who will still be paid, irrespective of the presence of the asset.
- *Revenue reduction from cannibalization.* If a proposed investment is intended to manufacture a product that is adjacent to one or more other products in a company's product line, there is a chance that the projected cash inflows will be offset to some extent by reductions in the sales of adjacent products that are being cannibalized.
- *Tax credits.* If an asset purchase triggers a tax credit (such as for a purchase of energy-reduction equipment), then note the amount of the credit.
- *Taxes.* Any income tax payments associated with net income expected to be derived from the asset. Also include any property taxes related to assets that are acquired.

- *Working capital*. If there will be an incremental change in the amount invested in accounts receivable or inventory as the result of a purchase decision, include these cash flows in the analysis. If the asset is to be eventually sold off, this may mean that the related working capital investment will be terminated at the same time, resulting in a positive surge in cash at some point in the future.

> **Note:** A possible consideration is what would be the incremental cost of a project if the government were to impose a carbon tax on an investment or the output from it. This could be a consideration when a project is expected to generate a significant amount of carbon dioxide over its useful life.

> **Note:** It is not acceptable to ignore working capital effects, even though they net to zero over the term of an investment. The problem is that there are negative cash flows associated with working capital near the beginning of an investment, which are only returned at the end of the investment, when the time value of money makes the returned working capital much less valuable.

All of the preceding factors should be considered when evaluating NPV for an investment proposal. In addition, consider generating several models to account for the worst case, most likely, and best case scenarios for cash flows.

Net present value is the traditional approach to evaluating capital expenditure proposals, since it is based on a single factor – cash flows – that can be used to judge any proposal arriving from anywhere in a company. However, this method can be a poor evaluation method if you suspect that the cash flows used to derive an analysis are incorrect. If so, consider using scenario analysis and sensitivity analysis to make a closer examination of the situation.

Scenario and Sensitivity Analysis

Scenario analysis involves the modeling of specific situations that can impact cash flows, such as the impact of an airliner crash on the willingness of the public to use air transport. Sensitivity analysis involves modeling worst-case and best-case changes in the key assumptions underlying an NPV analysis, such as market share or the costs of labor, utilities, and rent. These additional analyses are intended to note the extent to which cash flows may change. Here are several examples of the analyses that could be used for different types of capital expenditures:

- *Production equipment*. If equipment is being purchased to expand production capacity, use sensitivity analysis to examine the incremental increases in sales volume that are likely to be expected, with particular attention to the minimum amount of additional sales growth that must occur in order to generate enough cash flow to pay for the machinery.
- *Retail store*. Use sensitivity analysis to model seasonal sales levels to determine cash flows at different times of the year. Also use scenario analysis to

model for the impact of a direct competitor opening a store within a short distance of the proposed location.

- *Distribution facility.* Use sensitivity analysis to model the impact of changes in labor costs on the operation of the proposed facility, as well as changes in the cost of fuel to move inventory into and out of the proposed location.
- *Transportation service.* Examples of transportation services are ferries, cruise lines, airlines, and tour buses. Use scenario analysis to model the impact on cash flows of major accidents within the industry, increases in fuel costs due to Middle East conflicts, and changes in public concerns about disease transmission in public spaces.

EXAMPLE

Explorer Cruise Lines is contemplating the construction of a cruise ship that will circumnavigate Africa on an ongoing basis. The intent is to dock at major ports frequently, and send passengers inland on multi-day safaris. The initial analysis of potential cash flows indicates that this venture could be extremely profitable. However, a scenario analysis addresses the public's perception of pirates off the east coast of Africa, and the presence of the Ebola virus along the west coast, as well as political unrest along the north coast. All of these scenarios point toward the potential for massive declines in the number of paying passengers. Consequently, Explorer elects to restrict the proposed travel route to the South African and Namibian coastal regions, which are perceived to be safer.

Internal Rate of Return

The internal rate of return (IRR) is the rate of return at which the present value of a series of future cash flows equals the present value of all associated costs (that is, the discount rate at which the net present value of a project is zero). IRR is commonly used in capital budgeting to discern the rate of return on the estimated cash flows arising from an expected investment. The project having the highest IRR is selected for investment purposes.

The key benefit of using IRR is that the return on an investment is stated as a percentage, which can more easily be compared to the cost of capital to see if the cost of capital threshold has been matched or surpassed. If not, the investment will not generate a positive return, and so should be rejected.

The main flaw in the use of IRR for evaluating investment proposals is that it only focuses on the rate of return, not the size of the investment. For example, a proposed investment of $50,000 may have an IRR of 25%, while another investment of $200,000 has an IRR of 15%. If management can only pick one of the two proposals, which one should it pick? The smaller investment has a greater return on a percentage basis, but generates a smaller total amount of positive cash flow, since the investment is so much smaller. Management might select the project having the lower IRR, since doing so will employ a larger amount of cash and result in a greater gross return on investment.

The manual calculation of IRR can be time-consuming, since it involves guesstimating the appropriate discount factor from a present value table and gradually zeroing in on the correct figure. The easiest way to calculate the internal rate of return is to open Microsoft Excel and then follow these steps:

1. Enter in any cell a negative figure that is the amount of cash outflow in the first period. This is normal when acquiring fixed assets, since there is an initial expenditure to acquire and install the asset.

2. Enter the subsequent cash flows for each period following the initial expenditure in the cells immediately below the cell where the initial cash outflow figure was entered.

3. Access the IRR function and specify the cell range into which these entries were just made. The internal rate of return will be calculated automatically. It may be useful to use the Increase Decimal function to increase the number of decimal places appearing in the calculated internal rate of return.

As an example, a company is reviewing a possible investment for which there is an initial expected investment of $20,000 in the first year, followed by incoming cash flows of $12,000, $7,000 and $4,000 in the next three years. If this information is entered into the Excel IRR function, it returns an IRR of 8.965%.

Incremental Internal Rate of Return

The incremental internal rate of return is an analysis of the financial returns where there are two competing investment opportunities involving different amounts of investment. The analysis is applied to the difference between the costs of the two investments. Thus, subtract the cash flows associated with the less expensive alternative from the cash flows associated with the more expensive alternative to arrive at the cash flows applicable to the difference between the two alternatives, and then conduct an internal rate of return analysis on this difference.

Based just on quantitative analysis, select the more expensive investment opportunity if it has an incremental internal rate of return higher than the minimum return considered acceptable. However, there are qualitative issues to consider as well, such as whether there is an incremental increase in risk associated with the more expensive investment.

If you believe there is additional risk associated with the more expensive investment opportunity, then adjust for this risk by increasing the minimum return considered acceptable. For example, the minimum rate of return threshold for a low-risk investment might be 5%, while the threshold might be 10% for a high-risk investment.

EXAMPLE

Hassle Corporation is considering obtaining a color copier, and it can do so either with a lease or an outright purchase. The lease involves a series of payments over the three-year useful life of the copier, while the purchase option involves more cash up-front and some continuing maintenance, but it also has a resale value at the end of its useful life. The following analysis of the incremental differences in the cash flows between the two alternatives reveals that there is a positive incremental internal rate of return for the purchasing option. Barring any other issues (such as available cash to buy the copier), the purchasing option therefore appears to be the better alternative.

Year	Lease	Buy	Difference
0	-$7,000	-$29,000	-$22,000
1	-7,000	-1,500	5,500
2	-7,000	-1,500	5,500
3	-7,000	-1,500	5,500
Resale		+15,000	15,000
		Incremental IRR	13.3%

Terminal Value

The cash flows associated with an analysis may not have a discernible time horizon – that is, there is no expectation that they will end. In this case, it is customary to derive a terminal value, which is the aggregation of all cash flows beyond the date range for which cash flows are being predicted. Terminal value can be calculated with the *perpetuity formula*, which employs the following steps:

1. Estimate the cash flows associated with the final year of projections, and eliminate from this amount any unusual items that are not expected to occur again in later years.
2. Estimate a reasonable growth rate for this adjusted cash flow figure for later years. The amount should approximate the rate of growth for the entire economy. The rate of sustainable growth should be quite small, and may even be zero or a negative figure.
3. Subtract this growth rate from the company's weighted-average cost of capital (WACC), as derived in the Cost of Capital chapter, and divide the result into the adjusted cash flows for the final year. The formula is:

$$\frac{\text{Adjusted final year cash flow}}{\text{WACC} - \text{Growth rate}} = \text{Terminal value}$$

EXAMPLE

Glow Atomic is reviewing the projected income stream from a new type of fusion plant that could generate electricity in perpetuity. The analysis is broken into annual cash flows for the first 20 years, followed by a terminal value. The expected cash flow for the 20th year is $10,000,000. Glow expects these cash flows to increase at a rate of 1% thereafter. The company has a 15% WACC. Based on this information, the terminal value of the investment opportunity is:

$$\frac{\$10{,}000{,}000 \text{ final year cash flow}}{15\% \text{ WACC} - 1\% \text{ growth rate}} = \$71{,}429{,}000 \text{ Terminal value}$$

Profitability Index

The profitability index measures the acceptability of a proposed capital investment. It does so by comparing the initial investment to the present value of the future cash flows associated with that project. The formula is:

$$\frac{\text{Present value of future cash flows}}{\text{Initial investment}}$$

If the outcome of the ratio is greater than 1.0, this means that the present value of future cash flows to be derived from a project is greater than the amount of the initial investment. At least from a financial perspective, a score greater than 1.0 indicates that an investment should be made. As the score increases above 1.0, so too does the attractiveness of the investment. The ratio could be used to develop a ranking of projects, to determine the order in which available funds will be allocated to them.

For example, a financial analyst is reviewing a proposed investment that requires a $100,000 initial investment. At the company's standard discount rate, the present value of the cash flows expected from the project is $140,000. This results in a strong profitability index of 1.4, which would normally be accepted.

There are a number of other considerations besides the profitability index to examine when deciding whether to invest in a project. Other considerations include:

- *The availability of funds.* A business may not have access to sufficient funds to take advantage of all potentially profitable projects.
- *The perceived riskiness of the project.* A risk averse management team may turn down a project with a high profitability index if the associated risk of loss is too great.
- *Mutual exclusivity.* The index cannot be used to rank projects that are mutually exclusive; that is, only one investment or the other would be chosen, which is a binary solution. In this situation, a project with a large total net present value might be rejected if its profitability index were lower than that of a competing but much smaller project.

The profitability index is a variation on the net present value concept. The only difference is that it results in a ratio, rather than a specific number of dollars of net present value.

The Tax Rate

A cash flow analysis is deeply impacted by the income tax rate that a business pays, since cash inflows are reduced by the amount of income tax paid. A key issue when building a discounted cash flow analysis is what tax rate to use. The most theoretically correct tax rate is the marginal tax rate that will apply to a specific investment transaction. The logic behind using this rate is that the investment will result in an additional layer of income that would otherwise not exist, so the applicable tax rate will be the tax bracket in which the company finds itself after the investment has been made.

A concern with this logic is that a business is comprised of many income-producing activities, some of which are being scaled back while others are being introduced. In a larger organization with many of these activities, is it realistic to assign a specific tax rate to an individual project, or would it be better to use the expected tax rate for the applicable investment period? From the perspective of generating a simplified analysis, use of the expected tax rate for the entire business has a certain attraction.

Cash Flow Analysis Issues

The analyst should be aware of some issues that can reduce the accuracy of the cash flow information stated within an investment proposal. Here are some issues to consider:

- *Overlapping cash flows*. It is possible that the person originating an investment proposal has listed within it positive cash flows that are also being used as positive cash flows in a different investment proposal. If both proposals are accepted, the cash flows will not be duplicated, resulting in an aggregate amount of discounted cash flows that is lower than expected. The analyst can review all proposals relating to the same functional area of a business to see if any of these overlapping cash flows exist.
- *Overhead allocations*. The person preparing an investment proposal might mistakenly include an administrative or corporate overhead allocation in the negative cash flows portion of the analysis. Overhead costs will exist even in the absence of a proposed investment, and so should not be included in the proposal.

Summary

Discounted cash flow is one of the key tools used in the analysis of capital budget proposals. It places a distinct emphasis on the tracking of project cash flows, sometimes in minute detail. However, be aware of the large strategic issues noted in the preceding chapter, where management is deriving cash flow estimates based on its opinion of future competitive conditions. In some cases, a refined cash flow estimate may have little basis in reality, especially when the possible variability of future outcomes is large. Consequently, good judgment is critical when using discounted cash flow analysis.

Despite the preceding warning, many proposed investments do have predictable cash flows, especially those associated with existing products, product lines, customers, or distribution channels. In these cases, discounted cash flow analysis is a reliable tool for reviewing investment proposals.

Chapter 4
The Cost of Capital

Introduction

When a company makes a decision about how to invest its funds in various assets, part of the evaluation is based on the cost of those funds. This cost is known as the cost of capital. It is of some importance to be as precise as possible in deriving the cost of capital, since an incorrect measurement could lead to investments that yield excessively low returns, or foregone investments that would have generated returns in excess of the real cost of capital. In this chapter, we describe how the cost of capital is calculated and the ways in which the result can be skewed.

Cost of Capital Derivation

The cost of capital is the cost of funds for a business. Any investment of those funds must equal or exceed the cost of capital, or else investors in the business will experience a negative return on their investment, and the business may eventually fail.

The cost of capital is comprised of the cost of a company's debt, preferred stock, and common stock, which are then combined into a weighted average cost of capital. We will address the calculation of the cost of each of these components in this section at a simplified level, and then develop the concept in the following sections.

Cost of Debt

The cost of a company's debt is not just the average interest rate that it pays for all outstanding debt. Interest expense is tax-deductible, so reduce the interest rate by its tax impact. The calculation of the cost of debt is:

$$\frac{\text{Interest expense} \times (1 - \text{tax rate})}{\text{Amount of debt}} = \text{After-tax interest rate}$$

For example, if a company has $1,000,000 of outstanding debt at an interest rate of 6%, and its income tax rate is 21%, then its after-tax interest rate is:

$$\frac{\$60,000 \text{ interest expense} \times (1 - 21\% \text{ tax rate})}{\$1,000,000 \text{ of debt}} = 4.7\% \text{ after-tax interest rate}$$

Tip: If there are additional costs associated with debt, such as a placement fee, include this amount in the calculation of the interest rate being paid on the debt. The result will be a slight increase in the interest rate.

Cost of Preferred Stock

Preferred stock is the next component of the cost of capital. It is a form of equity that does not have to be repaid to the investor, but for which a dividend must be paid each year. This dividend is not tax-deductible to the company, so preferred stock is essentially a more expensive form of debt. The calculation of the cost of preferred stock is:

$$\frac{\text{Dividend expenditure}}{\text{Amount of preferred stock}} = \text{Preferred stock dividend rate}$$

For example, if a company has $2,000,000 of preferred stock that requires an annual dividend payment of $180,000, then the cost of the stock on a percentage basis is:

$$\frac{\$180,000 \text{ dividend expenditure}}{\$2,000,000 \text{ of preferred stock}} = 9\% \text{ preferred stock dividend rate}$$

Cost of Common Stock

The final component of the cost of capital is common stock, which is a more difficult calculation. The best way to calculate this cost is through the capital asset pricing model (CAPM). The CAPM is comprised of the following three elements:

1. The risk-free rate of return, which is usually considered the return on a U.S. government security.
2. The return on a group of securities considered to have an average risk level, such as the Standard & Poor's 500 or the Dow Jones Industrials. This is considered to be the premium that investors demand above the risk-free rate to invest in the stock market.
3. The beta of the company's stock, which defines the amount by which its stock returns vary from the returns of stocks having an average level of risk. A beta of 1.0 indicates average risk, while a higher figure indicates increased risk and a lower figure indicates reduced risk. Beta is available from a variety of research firms for most publicly-held companies.

The preceding component parts then plug into the following calculation of the cost of common stock:

$$\text{Risk-free return} + (\text{beta} \times (\text{average stock return} - \text{risk-free return})) = \text{Cost of common stock}$$

For example, if the risk-free return is 2%, the return on the Standard & Poor's 500 is 9%, and a company's beta is 1.2, the cost of its common stock would be:

$$2\% \text{ risk-free return} + (1.2 \text{ beta} \times (9\% \text{ average stock return} - 2\% \text{ risk-free return})) = 10.4\% \text{ cost of common stock}$$

If a company is privately-held, there will be no beta information for it. Instead, select a publicly-held firm that is operationally and financially similar to the company, and use the beta for this proxy firm. Better yet, use an average of the betas for several similar publicly-held firms, thereby avoiding the risk of using a comparative beta that represents an outlier value.

Weighted Average Cost of Capital

After the cost of each element of the cost of capital has been determined, calculate the weighted average cost of capital (WACC); this is based on the amount of common stock, preferred stock, and debt outstanding at the end of the most recent reporting period. The following table shows how to conduct the calculation. Note that the weighted average of the various elements of the cost of capital in the sample calculation is 12%, which would then be used for the discounted cash flow analysis of capital budgeting proposals.

Sample Cost of Capital Calculation

	Outstanding Amount	Interest Rate	Cost
Common stock	$10,000,000	15%	$1,500,000
Preferred stock	2,000,000	8%	160,000
Debt	4,500,000	7%	315,000
Totals	$16,500,000	12%	$1,975,000

This section has described the calculation of the WACC at a simplistic level. In the following two sections, we will describe how the inputs to the model can vary, and how the cost of capital can be adjusted for different situations.

Variations in the Cost of Capital

It can be quite difficult to derive an accurate cost of capital. This is not a minor issue, since the cost of capital is used to create discounted cash flow analyses for capital budgeting decisions. If the cost of capital is incorrect by even a small amount, this can alter management's decision to invest in a project. There are a number of ways in which the cost of capital may be incorrectly derived. For example, the following are all methods used to derive the cost of debt in the cost of capital formula:

- *The forecasted interest rate on the next new debt issuance.* This is the cost of the debt needed to fund the next round of capital projects, and so is the most relevant interest rate to include in the WACC formula.
- *The current average rate on debt outstanding.* This is the cost of debt needed to fund the *last* round of capital projects, which may not be applicable if interest rates have changed markedly in the meantime.

- *The historical rate of interest*. This may be the cost of debt that has been re-tired, and which may not have been applicable for the last few years.

There could be a particularly large difference between the historical and forecasted interest rate, which can result in a significant error in the derivation of the cost of capital. In most cases, the forecasted interest rate (which is the incremental rate) should be used.

A further error arises if the incorrect tax rate is used to derive the net cost of debt. The tax rate that should be used is the company's marginal tax rate that will apply to the specific investment transaction being contemplated. However, some organizations are more inclined to use their average tax rate, which could be significantly different.

The most difficult component of the cost of capital to calculate is the cost of equity, which means that this cost is the most likely to be wrong. Consider the following points:

- *Risk-free rate*. The risk-free rate is an input used to derive the cost of equity; but what is the risk-free rate? Most organizations use the interest rate on U.S. Treasury bonds as a proxy for the risk-free rate, but there is no agreement on which bond. The instruments chosen typically vary from the 90-day bill to the 30-year bond, which presents a wide range of interest rates. Further, some organizations derive an *average* rate from instruments having different maturities, while others may choose to use a *forecasted* U.S. Treasury rate. There may also be inconsistency in using different U.S. Treasury instruments over time.
- *Stock market premium*. The additional return over the risk-free rate that investors demand in order to invest in the stock market is also used to derive the cost of equity. There is a wide range in the assumed amount of this return. Once selected, companies are not in the habit of adjusting the rate, even though there may be changes over time in the comparative level of turmoil in the financial markets that would warrant an adjustment.
- *Beta*. Beta is the amount of variability in the value of a company's stock in comparison to the market. The level of beta will change over time, so there is an issue with the historical time period over which beta should be calculated. A short-duration calculation period may happen to include a radical swing in a company's stock price, which would trigger a high beta. However, a very long-term time horizon would tend to downplay any recent stock price volatility. Thus, the time period covered by the calculation can cause major differences in a company's beta, and therefore in its cost of capital.

We have thus far identified a variety of ways to modify the outcome of the components of the cost of capital. In addition, the assumptions used to assemble these components into a weighted average cost of capital can also result in different outcomes. The most common basis for deriving the WACC is to weight the components based on the book values of debt and equity.

However, some organizations elect to derive the weighting based on one of these other methods:

- The targeted amounts of debt and equity that will be on the books as of a later date
- The current market values of debt and equity
- The current market value of debt and the book value of equity
- The book value of debt and the current market value of equity

Ideally, the current market values of debt and equity should be used to derive the WACC, since this most accurately reflects the current expectations of investors regarding the funding mix that the company employs. If management expects that the current round of funding will notably alter the mix of debt and equity, then it can incorporate these changes into its use of the current market values of debt and equity.

It may be acceptable to derive the WACC using the book value of debt, if the company is not expecting to obtain additional debt financing. In this case, the amount recorded on the books is indeed the company's actual cost of debt. The same cannot be said for the cost of equity, which is constantly changing as investors bid the price of a company's stock up or down in accordance with their current expectations for a return on investment.

The method chosen can lead to major differences in the weighting of the debt and equity components of the cost of capital. The problem is especially apparent when a business is in financial difficulties and at least one element of the weighting is based on market value, since the market value is likely to be far less than book value. The following example illustrates the issue.

EXAMPLE

Creekside Industrial issued debt and stock to the public five years ago, after which it has reported reduced financial results that have led investors to believe that the company will have difficulty surviving as an independent business. The result has been a significant decline in the market value of its debt and equity. However, since the bonds payable are classified as senior debt, investors have a reasonable chance of obtaining repayment, so the bonds have retained their value better than the components of equity.

Creekside's CFO is now engaged in a review of the company's cost of capital. She creates the following table, which reveals the book value and market value of its funding sources, as well as their relative proportions:

(000s)	Book Value	Proportion of Total	Market Value	Proportion of Total
Bonds payable	$23,000	30%	$19,000	63%
Preferred stock	11,000	15%	3,000	10%
Common stock	42,000	55%	8,000	27%
Totals	$76,000	100%	$30,000	100%

Based on this information, the CFO derives the following weighted average cost of capital, based separately on book value and market value, which shows a significant 1.9% difference when the market values of debt and equity are employed.

	Book Value Weighting			Market Value Weighting		
	Cost	Weighting	Extended	Cost	Weighting	Extended
Bonds payable	6.0%	30%	1.8%	6.0%	63%	3.8%
Preferred stock	9.5%	15%	1.4%	9.5%	10%	1.0%
Common stock	12.5%	55%	6.9%	12.5%	27%	3.4%
Totals		100%	**10.1%**		100%	**8.2%**

The points made in this section should make it clear that achieving a precise cost of capital is difficult, given the extent to which assumptions can skew the measure. Consequently, it is important to clarify the assumptions used in the derivation of the cost of capital and to update the calculation on a regular basis. Otherwise, an incorrect cost of capital will likely lead to non-optimal investment decisions.

Adjustments to the Cost of Capital

Even after the cost of capital has been derived, questions may be raised concerning when to use it, and when to adjust it. Consider the following situations:

- *Multi-unit business.* A larger corporation may have a number of operating units, each of which operates in environments with different risk characteristics. It may be tempting to derive a separate cost of capital for each of these units, but the calculation requires that each one acquire its own debt and have its shares publicly traded, which is rarely the case for a subsidiary. An alternative is to estimate what the cost of capital would be, based on a mix of comparable companies that are publicly held, and which operate primarily in the same markets as the subsidiary. The result will not be precise, but could yield a better indication of the real cost of capital than the corporate rate.
- *Single investment.* What if funding is being obtained for a specific investment? For example, a utility issues bonds specifically to build a power plant. In this case, the after-tax cost of the debt used to buy the power plant should be considered the cost of capital for the purpose of making an investment decision about that specific project, rather than the weighted average cost of capital for the entire business.
- *Foreign investment.* What if a multi-national company wants to make an investment in a foreign location? One option is to use the cost of capital for the entire company, since a multi-national is comprised of a portfolio of investments (subsidiaries), which result in an aggregated portfolio risk that can be applied to investments everywhere. If this approach is used, it may be necessary to adjust the cost of capital for any relative difference in the inflation rate

between the home and foreign currency. Another option is to derive a local cost of capital, on the grounds that each country has its own environmental factors, such as political risks and tax policy that can strongly influence the rate of return within that country. A third option is to apply a risk premium to the corporate cost of capital that is based on the risk factors in the foreign market. This risk premium is considered to be the interest rate on bonds issued by the foreign government, minus the interest rate on a risk-free bond issued by the home government, adjusted for the difference in the inflation rates of the home and foreign currencies.

- *Lending inefficiencies*. There may be times when it is difficult to obtain funds from a lender at a reasonable rate of interest, no matter how excellent a company's credit history may be. If so and there is variable-rate debt outstanding, the cost of capital should include the most recent interest rate, since that is the rate being charged to the company. Even if there is an expectation of a later decline in the interest rate, the only factual representation of the interest rate is the current inflated rate, which will apply to investments made in the near future.
- *Future expectations*. The beta component of the cost of equity is based on the historical results of a business. Management may feel that this beta figure is not valid, since it expects different results for the company in the future. However, the expectations of management do not always translate into actual results. Also, the market may continue to assign roughly the same beta to the company, simply because of the industry in which it is located. For these reasons, it is better to continue to use the existing beta, perhaps with a weighting that favors the most recent beta for the past year.

Cost of Capital as a Threshold Value

The primary use of the cost of capital is, as the name implies, to establish a cost for the funds that a business employs. Thus, if management is considering the acquisition of a fixed asset, it can judge the acquisition by comparing its projected return on investment to the cost of capital. If the projected return is less than the cost of capital, then the acquisition should be rejected, on the grounds that the cost of the funds required to buy the asset will exceed the return expected from the investment.

Given the variability in the calculation of the cost of capital, as noted earlier, some managers are reluctant to rely upon it as a decision threshold. Instead, they may arbitrarily add several percentage points onto the cost of capital and use the result as the threshold for investment decisions. The reasons for doing so include:

- The higher rate allows for any errors that may have been incorporated into the cost of capital.
- The higher rate allows for any errors in the derivation of the capital budgeting proposals being judged.
- The higher rate acknowledges the existence of some investments that have no return at all (such as to meet regulatory requirements), so that other

investments must generate a higher return in order to arrive at an average return for all investments that exceeds the cost of capital.

However, arbitrarily adding a few percentage points to the cost of capital reduces the level of quantitative rigor used to evaluate an investment. A better approach is to recognize what the upper and lower boundaries of the cost of capital may be, and to review investment proposals based on these two values.

The cost of capital may also be adjusted based on the perceived risk of a proposed investment. For example, the threshold value may be the cost of capital when a proposed investment pertains to an existing product line, but the threshold is increased by 5% if the investment is for an entirely new product in an untested market. This approach can be used to incorporate a high level of conservatism into the evaluation of riskier projects. However, at some point management must consciously invest in the strategic direction of the business, rather than relying upon quantitative measures to tell it where to spend money. For such strategic decisions, many other factors than the cost of capital must be considered, including the level of competition, government regulations, technology issues, and the perceived duration of any market opportunities.

It is possible to apply a different risk-adjusted cost of capital percentage to different elements of a cash flow analysis for a single investment. Doing so recognizes that there are different risks associated with different cash flows. For example, a significant investment is proposed for a product line, where the expected inflow of cash from the domestic market is essentially guaranteed, because there is an established market for it. The proposal also includes a separate set of cash flows from sales of the product in a different country, where there is no cultural acceptance of the product. Given the situation, there is a much higher probability that the second set of cash flows will not materialize, so it could make sense to apply a higher discount rate to them. Following this logic, it might be reasonable to parse the cash flows related to a larger investment proposal, and apply a different discount rate to each one.

Summary

This chapter showed how easy it is to derive a cost of capital that is excessively high or low, depending on the assumptions used in the calculation. The cost of capital is a key component of discounted cash flow analysis, so be sure to spend as much time as possible questioning every aspect of the derived cost of capital. Hopefully, a rigorous review will yield a value that requires minimal inflation to guard against a mistake. Also, it is entirely possible that only a range of values can be derived for the cost of capital, rather than a single figure. If so, it may be necessary to use this range of values when examining investment alternatives, which may make it difficult to reach a purely quantitative decision.

Chapter 5
Constraint Analysis

Introduction

In the traditional management environment, suggestions for improvements trickle in from all departments, which the management team must sort through and decide whether to implement. It can be quite difficult to achieve a perfect cause-and-effect, where an investment in one part of the business indisputably causes an improvement in profits. More commonly, a change has a ripple effect in other areas that may have a net positive or negative impact on profits. Constraint analysis provides for a cleaner decision-making environment, since profits are primarily improved by focusing on the constraint, as well as on selective cost reductions that do not impact the constraint.

> **Related Podcast Episode:** Episode 45 of the Accounting Best Practices Podcast discusses throughput capital expenditures. It is available at: **accountingtools.com/podcasts** or **iTunes**

The Bottleneck Operation

The key assumption underlying the traditional view of management is that a number of operations have a notable impact on the ability of a business to generate a profit. This means that multiple operations must be optimized. However, constraint analysis throws out this concept, instead stating that just one operation (the constraint, also known as the bottleneck or constrained resource) drives the ability of an entire business to generate a profit. The concept of a single constraint on the entire system is shown in the following example, where the production capacity of one workstation limits the capacity of the entire production system.

EXAMPLE

Pensive Corporation manufactures the Procrastinator Deluxe, a robot used to save labor around the house. The production process involves work at four workstations. The following base case shows that Workstation C can process the fewest units per hour, at 60 units. This constrains the processing speed of the entire operation, resulting in total output of 60 units per hour.

Base Case:

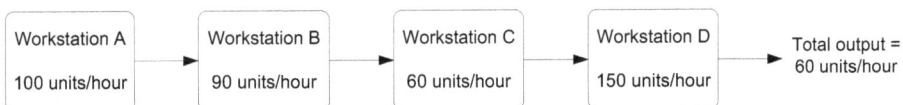

The company's financial analyst conducts an incorrect analysis and recommends that the machines used in Workstations A and B be replaced by higher-capacity equipment. This is done, with the result appearing in the following process flow:

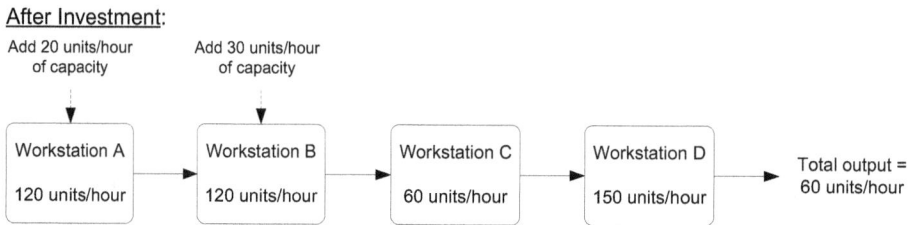

After Investment:

Add 20 units/hour of capacity	Add 30 units/hour of capacity			
▼	▼			
Workstation A 120 units/hour	→ **Workstation B** 120 units/hour	→ **Workstation C** 60 units/hour	→ **Workstation D** 150 units/hour	→ Total output = 60 units/hour

The results are unchanged, since the higher production volume of the first two workstations is still limited by Workstation C. The only changes are that the company has invested in enhanced equipment that it does not need, and which generate an increased amount of inventory that is piling up in front of Workstation C, waiting to be processed.

This constraint must be carefully managed to ensure that it is operational as close to round-the-clock as possible. If not, profitability will suffer. The management of all other aspects of the organization is of much less concern than the management of the constraint.

Under the constraints view, optimizing all operations only means that it is easier to generate more inventory that will pile up in front of the constraint, without profits increasing. Thus, widespread optimization merely leads to the creation of more inventory, rather than more profits.

EXAMPLE

Global Camper is a manufacturer of motorhomes. Its constrained operation is its paint shop. Painting operations can only proceed at a certain pace, so the company can only run 25 tractors per day through the facility. If the company were to produce more engines, the engines would not contribute to more tractors being built; there would only be an increase in the number of engines in storage, which increases the investment in working capital.

The president of the company finds that, since the number of tractors produced per day is limited to 25, his next best activity is to cut back production in all other areas if they are producing more parts than are needed for 25 tractors. Thus, it is better to not optimize in many parts of the business, since there is no need for more parts.

In short, the key points in understanding constraint analysis are as follows:

1. A company is an integrated set of processes that function together to generate a profit; and
2. There is a chokepoint somewhere in a company that absolutely controls its ability to earn a profit.

Constraint Analysis

Under constraint analysis, the key concept is that an entire company acts as a single system, which generates a profit. Under this concept, capital expenditures revolve around the following logic:

1. Nearly all of the costs of the production system do not vary with individual sales; that is, nearly every cost is an operating expense (all costs other than totally variable costs); therefore,
2. It is necessary to maximize the throughput (revenues minus totally variable costs) of the *entire* system in order to pay for the operating expense; and
3. The only way to increase throughput is to maximize the throughput passing through the bottleneck operation.

Consequently, give primary consideration to those capital expenditure proposals that favorably impact the throughput passing through the bottleneck operation.

From the perspective of constraint management, the only capital investments that should be made in a business are ones that will either increase throughput or reduce operating expenses. When this priority is assigned to capital requests, it is entirely likely that an organization will be able to avoid a number of asset purchases. The following asset requests can be avoided:

1. *Local optimization.* A request may be to increase the efficiency of a workstation that does nothing to increase throughput. If so, the investment is wasted, since the company invests funds and receives no return on its investment.
2. *Sprint capacity increase.* Sprint capacity is excess production capacity positioned upstream from the bottleneck operation. It is needed to ensure that inventory can be rushed to the bottleneck operation to keep it functioning at all times. A request may involve an increase in sprint capacity. If so, review the request to see if the size of the capacity increase is reasonable, based on the company's expectations for the amount of sprint capacity needed.
3. *Constraint capacity increase.* What if a proposed investment *is* designed to increase the capacity of the constraint? If so, compare the projected amount of incremental new capacity to the projected amount of capacity needed to fulfill throughput requirements. It is entirely possible that the investment will create too much capacity, which merely shifts the constraint to a different location in the company. The appropriate response is to scale back the amount of the investment to only build the required amount of additional capacity.
4. *Expense reduction.* If a capital request is not addressed by the preceding review steps, this means the only remaining justification is that the investment will reduce operating expenses. If so, subject the request to an especially detailed review, with a particular emphasis on the assumptions used to prove that expenses will indeed be reduced. Unless there is a high probability of an adequate expense reduction *and* a low probability of a cost overrun on the investment, reject the request.

The decision to increase the capacity of the constrained resource is a particularly important one. This resource is likely to be the constraint in the system precisely because it is quite expensive to increase the capacity level. Consequently, investments in this area require a considerable amount of investigation. A possible outcome is that these types of investments are delayed until such time as management has accumulated more information about the likelihood of future changes in capacity requirements.

The Inventory Buffer

There will always be flaws in the production process that result in variability in the flow of materials to the constrained resource. This means that there will always be periods when there is no inventory to feed into the constraint, so that the constraint will not be used. This issue is dealt with by building up a buffer of inventory in front of the bottleneck operation. In the following sub-sections, we deal with several buffer issues.

Buffer Sizing

If ongoing industrial engineering efforts have succeeded in reducing inconsistencies in the flow of goods to the bottleneck, the constraint buffer can be relatively small. Conversely, if there is still wide variability in the flow of parts to the bottleneck, it will be necessary to protect the constraint with quite a large inventory buffer.

The existence of a large buffer is particularly important if a company does not have a sufficient amount of excess capacity upstream from the constraint, since these upstream operations will not be able to easily build up a surge of new parts to rebuild the buffer in the event that the buffer is depleted (also known as a buffer penetration). In this case, a production snafu may clear out most of the buffer, and then put the business at risk of another constraint shutdown during the extended period when the buffer is being slowly rebuilt back to its former size.

A large buffer cannot substitute for the addition of production capacity to upstream workstations, especially since it takes lots of excess capacity to build the buffer in the first place. Ideally, there should be sufficient available capacity to rebuild the buffer in short order, if a production snafu requires that inventory be withdrawn from the buffer.

The amount of upstream capacity needed to initially build and then maintain an inventory buffer does not necessarily require an inordinate investment, if a proper analysis is conducted to determine the exact amounts of additional capacity needed. The correct amount of capacity can be determined over time by gradually increasing the capacity level in response to actual buffer penetrations, or by modeling such penetrations to see where capacity needs to be bolstered. Another option is to increase capacity in those areas where labor is needed, rather than fixed assets, by engaging in extensive cross-training and then calling in the extra staff when there is a sudden need to increase production volume.

EXAMPLE

Sharper Designs manufactures knives for chefs. The company's facility is located in a flood plain, and the shop floor was recently inundated with flood waters for two days, rendering the facility inoperable. The constraint, a manual knife handle carving operation, continued to run on the second floor of the building, and soon ran out of work when there were no more knife blades arriving from the upstream (no pun intended) operations located on the first floor. The president of Sharper faces the following choices:

- *Continue as before.* The president accepts the fact that floods will interrupt operations from time to time, and does nothing new to guard against it. This approach is a reasonable one if floods are a rare occurrence.
- *Install levees.* The company can build levees around its perimeter, so that floodwater up to a certain depth cannot enter the facility. This approach is feasible if there is a reasonable probability of recurring floods, and the amount of lost throughput offsets the cost of the levees.
- *Create inventory buffer.* The company can invest in a sufficient amount of knife blade inventory buffer to protect against the expected amount of downtime caused by a flooding event. This assumes that the flooding will not be so bad that constraint operations cannot continue on the second floor.
- *Build upstream capacity.* Invest in more metal fabrication equipment, so that the flow of knife blades to the knife handle carving operation is not significantly interrupted. This could work if combined with a sufficient inventory buffer to last through the expected duration of a flood. However, an additional concern is that the extra equipment could be damaged by floodwaters.

If the probability of additional flooding is high, another consideration for the president is to move the entire facility away from the flood plain, to higher ground.

The preceding example shows that there are many viable alternatives for management to sort through, each of which optimizes the situation under different circumstances.

Sprint Capacity

Sprint capacity is an excess amount of production capacity located upstream from the constrained resource, possibly in several different workstations. The intent of having sprint capacity is to ensure that any inventory shortages at the constraint can be rapidly refilled.

Sprint capacity can be expensive to incorporate into a production process, especially when it involves acquiring production equipment. In other cases where additional capacity mostly involves adding additional staff to a work area for a short period of time, additions are less of an issue. In either case, the best way to add sprint capacity is based on an analysis of inventory shortfalls in the past, and determining the amount of extra capacity that would have been needed to overcome those prior shortages.

Sprint capacity cannot involve outsourced capacity, unless suppliers have remarkably fast reaction speeds. In most cases, the usual delay of several days in receiving ordered parts from suppliers makes this alternative impractical.

Local Optimization

The concept of the constraint is very much at odds with the traditional concept of local optimization, where everyone works to improve the efficiency of every operation throughout a company. In many cases, these improvements do nothing to increase overall company profits, because the primary driver of profits is still the constrained resource. Consequently, if there are investments in local optimization projects, profits do not improve, but the investment in the company increases, so the only logical outcome is that the aggregate return on investment declines. The following table contains several examples of how constraint analysis alters one's view of local optimization.

Constraint Analysis Solutions

Situation	Local Optimization Solution	Constraint Analysis Solution
Overtime is 10% of payroll	Restrict all overtime	Do not restrict overtime if it is being spent on the bottleneck operation, or on any operations feeding the bottleneck
A machine is not being utilized	Sell the machine	Keep the machine if it provides sprint capacity for the bottleneck operation
A product can be redesigned	Only do so if the product is at the end of its normal life cycle	Do so if the redesign reduces the product processing time at the bottleneck operation
The production staff is not fully utilized	Cut back on operations and lay off staff	If there is no bottleneck operation, lower prices to attract more sales
A machine is reaching its maximum utilization	Buy an additional machine	Only buy an additional unit if it will provide more sprint capacity. Do not buy if it is located downstream from the bottleneck operation
A supplier is asking us to outsource production	Do so if it passes a cost-benefit analysis	Do so if it reduces the load on the bottleneck operation

In all of the cases noted in the table, it is necessary to step back from the individual decision and see what the impact will be on the entire company before determining the correct course of action.

In particular, be aware of two problems that are caused by local optimization:

1. *Excess inventory.* If a production operation is optimized that is not the constraint, all that has been done is give it the ability to churn out even more inventory than was previously the case, and which the constraint will be unable to process. Thus, you have not only needlessly invested in the operation, but also needlessly invested in additional inventory that must now wait to be processed.
2. *Overly efficient labor.* When a good manufacturing process was considered to be one with very long production runs, there was a considerable emphasis on highly efficient labor. If there is instead a focus on maximizing the amount of production passing through the constraint – and nowhere else – it is reasonable to grossly overstaff the constraint to make sure that it is always operating, and pay much less attention to labor efficiencies elsewhere. Employees should only work if inventory is actually needed. In short, it is better to have

employees be underutilized and produce less inventory than to be more efficient and produce inventory that is not needed.

In summary, a company does not even have to be especially efficient in production areas located away from the constraint. Instead, the one and only focus is on maximizing the efficiency of the bottleneck. This change in focus alters most of the decisions that would be reached if one were to only focus on local optimization.

Investment Decision Priorities

The management team is likely to receive a variety of recommendations for improvements. What are the main criteria for how to prioritize these proposals? The proper ranking is as noted in the following sub-sections, where we place a strong emphasis on projects that increase throughput, with a lesser emphasis on activities that will either reduce the amount of invested funds or the amount of expenses incurred.

Priority 1 – Increases Throughput

If a proposed action will increase total throughput, this recommendation always has first priority. The reason for giving this the highest status is that there is no upward cap on throughput – it can potentially increase forever, so the potential profits to be gained are the largest. For example, a proposal to add a shift at the bottleneck operation will increase throughput, and so should probably be approved, subject to an analysis of the amount of throughput that will be realized and the offsetting amount of the cost.

Proposals to increase throughput typically involve an additional expenditure, rather than an expense reduction, since some investment is usually required to expand the ability to generate throughput. It is a rare proposal indeed that can reduce expenses while *increasing* throughput.

Proposals that contain any of the following outcomes are more likely to increase throughput, and so should be considered favorably:

- Faster delivery times can be promised to customers, for which they are willing to pay a higher price
- The feature set of the product or service will be enriched, and this change can be used to increase prices
- The feature will increase customer involvement, thereby triggering repeat business
- The usage level of the constrained resource will increase, subject to any additional expenditures related to excessive usage levels
- Total revenue will increase, net of sales returns and bad debts

Priority 2 – Reduces Invested Funds

When a proposal involves reducing the amount of invested funds, this is given a secondary priority after throughput-generating activities. The reason is that there is only a certain amount of funding that can be stripped out of a business, so there is a hard cap on this type of activity. Further, unless very carefully conducted, a reduction in invested funds can have a negative impact on the throughput generating capacity of a business.

An example of a useful reduction in invested funds is the elimination of production equipment associated with a production line that has been terminated. In this case, there is no possible use for the equipment to support other product lines, so retaining the investment would be wasteful. Conversely, the tightening of customer credit in order to reduce the investment in accounts receivable may be a more dangerous reduction of invested funds. The reason is that the more marginal customers that will be turned away under this policy might be generating positive throughput for the company, even if they have a heightened risk of causing bad debts.

An area commonly targeted for a reduction of invested funds is inventory. Inventory reductions can have a mixed impact on the ability to generate throughput. If a reduction is used to shrink the number of jobs residing on the shop floor, this can have quite a positive effect, since it is easier to move goods through the production area, and it is easier to prioritize the remaining jobs. However, if inventory is removed from the buffer in front of the constraint, the result can be a sharp decline in throughput. Consequently, inventory reduction must be carefully planned before any changes are enacted.

Proposals that contain any of the following outcomes are more likely to reduce the amount of invested funds, and so should be considered favorably:

- The investment in accounts receivable can be reduced, subject to the impact on lost sales
- The investment in any type of inventory can be reduced, subject to the impact on the inventory buffer
- The investment in fixed assets can be reduced, subject to the impact on the ability to generate throughput

Priority 3 – Reduces Expenses

The lowest priority is to eliminate or reduce expenses. As was the case with the reduction of invested funds, there is an upper cap on the amount of expenses that can be eliminated, so this is simply not as target-rich an environment as activities that can increase throughput. In addition, expense reductions frequently have either a direct or indirect negative impact on an organization's ability to generate throughput. For these reasons, proposed expense reductions are given the lowest priority.

An example of a harmful expense reduction is a blanket prohibition on the use of overtime, since extra working hours may be needed to ensure that the bottleneck operation is being operated at the highest possible level. Areas in which expense reductions are likely to have less impact on throughput include administration and corporate-level expenses.

Proposals that contain any of the following outcomes are more likely to reduce expenses, and so should be considered favorably:

- Raw material costs can be reduced, subject to the impact of any lower-quality materials on the constraint
- Operating expenses can be reduced, as long as there is no impact on the ability to generate throughput

Additional Investment Considerations

In the last section, we noted the basic priority system for improvement projects. In this section, we continue with the topic, but now focus on additional concepts that should be considered as part of an investment decision.

One concern is the projected demand for a company's products. The typical product life cycle contains steep initial sales growth, after which sales flatten and then eventually decline. Depending on the stage in the product life cycle and the mix of products being manufactured, it should be possible to make a rough estimate of the likely overall level of demand in the near future, and the impact this will have on the constraint. It is entirely possible that sales projections are relatively flat, in which case any additional investments may be minimal. In this situation, even investments in the constraint may be imprudent, since the result is an incremental increase in capacity that will never be used.

A variation on the last concept is when the level of demand grows quite slowly, perhaps at a rate of just a few percent a year. In this situation, the demand on the constraint is very gradually increasing, while the amount of available sprint capacity is slowly shrinking, as slight increases in customer orders slowly soak up excess upstream capacity. Eventually, this means that the amount of sprint capacity will drop so low that it will take a long time to rebuild the buffer inventory following a large buffer penetration. This situation must be guarded against by watching excess capacity levels on a trend line throughout the upstream workstations, and being willing to invest at intervals to ensure that sprint capacity levels are always sufficient.

What if a company is located in an industry that is subject to sudden, unexpected spikes in sales, as is common in the fashion industry? In this situation, sales may be lost if orders are not filled at once, so there is a need for a large amount of excess capacity. Also, this demand probably cannot be offloaded to a supplier, since the demand period is so short. If these demand spikes are associated with highly profitable goods (again, as is common in the fashion industry) it can make sense to invest heavily in excess capacity, even though that capacity may not be used most of the time.

The Constraint Analysis Model

Thomas Corbett developed an excellent constraint analysis model, which is outlined here. The basic thrust of the model is to give priority in the constraint to those products that generate the highest throughput per minute of constraint time. After these products are manufactured, priority is then given to the product having the next highest throughput per minute, and so on. Eventually, the production queue is filled, and the operation can accept no additional work.

The key element in the model is the use of throughput per minute, because the key limiting factor in a constraint is time – hence, maximizing throughput within the shortest possible time frame is paramount. Note that throughput *per minute* is much more important than total throughput *per unit*. The following example illustrates the point.

EXAMPLE

Mole Industries manufactures trench digging equipment. It has two products with different amounts of throughput and processing times at the constrained resource. The key information about these products is:

Product	Total Throughput	Constraint Processing Time	Throughput per Minute
Mole Hole Digger	$400	2 minutes	$200
Mole Driver Deluxe	800	8 minutes	100

Of the two products, the Mole Driver Deluxe creates the most overall throughput, but the Mole Hole Digger creates more throughput per minute of constraint processing time. To determine which one is more valuable to Mole Industries, consider what would happen if the company had an unlimited order quantity of each product, and could run the constrained resource non-stop, all day (which equates to 1,440 minutes). The operating results would be:

Product	Throughput per Minute		Total Processing Time Available		Total Throughput
Mole Hole Digger	$200	×	1,440 minutes	=	$288,000
Mole Driver Deluxe	100	×	1,440 minutes	=	144,000

Clearly, the Mole Hole Digger, with its higher throughput per minute, is much more valuable to Mole Industries than its Mole Driver Deluxe product. Consequently, the company should push sales of the Mole Hole Digger product whenever possible.

The constraint analysis model is essentially a production plan that itemizes the amount of throughput that can be generated, as well as the total amount of operating expenses and investment. In the sample model, we use four different products, each requiring some processing time in the constraint. The columns in the model are as follows:

- *Throughput per minute.* This is the total amount of throughput that a product generates, divided by the amount of processing time at the constrained resource.

- *Constraint usage.* This is the number of minutes of processing time required by a product at the constrained resource. This figure is the sum total of both the setup time for a job and the actual run time for the job.
- *Units scheduled.* This is the number of units scheduled to be processed at the constrained resource.
- *Total constraint time.* This is the total number of minutes of processing time required by a product, multiplied by the number of units to be processed.
- *Total throughput.* This is the throughput per minute multiplied by the number of units processed at the constrained resource.

This grid produces a total amount of throughput to be generated if production proceeds according to plan. Below the grid of planned production, there is a subtotal of the total amount of throughput, from which the total amount of operating expenses are subtracted to arrive at the amount of profit. Finally, the total amount of investment in assets is divided into the profit to calculate the return on investment. Thus, the model provides a complete analysis of all three ways in which you can improve the results of a company – increase throughput, decrease operating expenses, or increase the return on investment. An example of the model follows:

Sample Constraint Analysis Model

Product	Throughput per Minute	Constraint Usage (minutes)	Units Scheduled	Total Constraint Time	Total Throughput
1. Hedgehog Deluxe	$80	14	1,000	14,000	$1,120,000
2. Hedgehog Mini	70	20	500	10,000	700,000
3. Hedgehog Classic	65	40	200	8,000	520,000
4. Hedgehog Digger	42	10	688	6,880	288,960
		Total constraint scheduled time		38,880	
		Total constraint time available*		38,880	
			Total throughput		$2,628,960
			Total operating expenses		2,400,000
			Profit		$228,960
			Profit percentage		8.7%
			Investment		$23,000,000
			Annualized return on investment		11.9%

* Minutes per month = 30 days × 24 hours × 60 minutes × $(1 - 0.10$ maintenance time)

In the example, the Hedgehog Deluxe product has the largest throughput per minute, and so is scheduled to be the first priority for production. The Hedgehog Digger has the lowest throughput per minute, so it is given last priority in the production schedule. If there is less time available on the constrained resource, the company should reduce the number of the Hedgehog Digger product manufactured in order to maximize overall profits.

In the middle of the model, the "Total constraint scheduled time" row contains the total number of minutes of scheduled production. The row below it, labeled "Total constraint time available," represents the total estimate of time that the constraint should have available for production purposes during the scheduling period. Since the time scheduled and available are identical, this means that the production schedule has completely maximized the availability of the constrained resource.

One calculation anomaly in the model is that the profit percentage is normally calculated as profit divided by revenues. However, since revenues are not included in the model, we instead use profits divided by throughput. Since throughput is less than revenue, we are overstating the profit percentage as compared to the traditional profit percentage calculation.

Use the constraint analysis model in a before-and-after mode, to see what effect a proposed change will have on profitability or the return on investment. If the model improves as a result of a change, then implement the change. In the next section, we will examine how the constraint analysis model is used to arrive at several management decisions.

Note: We will continue to use this model through the remainder of the chapter, retaining the information just noted in the sample model as the baseline scenario. An important point in the following analyses is the assumption that the company can continue to produce more units of the Hedgehog Digger product, which is listed as the least profitable product in the table.

Production Analysis

There are numerous analyses that one can engage in related to the treatment of a constraint in the production area. In this section, we describe the analyses for changing capacity levels at several points in the product process, increasing upstream processing, and shifting work outside of the company.

Increase Downstream Capacity

When an organization uses local optimization, the assumption is that profitable improvements can be made to every aspect of the business. If this faulty approach to management is prevalent, it will be quite common for suggestions to be made to invest in those parts of a business that are not the constraint, and which do not support the constraint. For example, a proposed investment location may be downstream from the constraint. In this area, any increase in capacity will be wasted, since the flow of parts into that location will be restricted by the output of the constrained resource.

The analysis of any such proposal is fairly easy, since there is no impact on the amount of throughput already being processed. Instead, the only impact is on the amount of money invested in the operation, which increases. Since the only change in the model is an increased investment, the only logical outcome of the investment decision is that the return on investment will decline. The concept is noted in the following example.

EXAMPLE

The industrial engineering staff of Mole Industries has just finished conducting a comprehensive examination of the entire production process, and has concluded that there is a serious opportunity for improvement in the paint booth area. The paint booth is located near the end of the production process, well after the constraint operation. The recommended improvement is to invest $250,000 in new technology that automatically cleans the paint nozzles in the paint booth, so that the paint staff does not have to shut down the booth each day to conduct cleaning operations. This change will increase the capacity of the paint booth by 30%.

The company's skeptical financial analyst realizes that this investment will not increase output at all, since the quantity of products arriving at the paint booth will not change. Accordingly, she adds the proposed $250,000 investment to the existing $23,000,000 investment used in the corporate throughput model. The only change to the model (noted in bold) is that the return on investment declines from 11.9% to 11.8%. The analysis is:

Product	Throughput per Minute	Constraint Usage (minutes)	Units Scheduled	Total Constraint Time	Total Throughput
1. Hedgehog Deluxe	$80	14	1,000	14,000	$1,120,000
2. Hedgehog Mini	70	20	500	10,000	700,000
3. Hedgehog Classic	65	40	200	8,000	520,000
4. Hedgehog Digger	42	10	688	6,880	288,960
		Total constraint scheduled time		38,880	
		Total constraint time available*		38,880	
			Total throughput		$2,628,960
			Total operating expenses		2,400,000
			Profit		$228,960
			Profit percentage		8.7%
			Investment		**$23,250,000**
			Annualized return on investment		**11.8%**

* Minutes per month = 30 days × 24 hours × 60 minutes × (1 − 0.10 maintenance time)

The analyst, somewhat crotchety from not yet having imbibed her morning coffee, suggests that a better investment would be to send the industrial engineering staff to a constraint management class.

There are some types of investment that can make sense, even if they are not associated with the constraint. In particular, if an investment can reduce the cost of an operation, the investment is acceptable, as long as the return on investment percentage increases as a result of the change. The concept is illustrated in the following example.

EXAMPLE

Rather than proposing a capacity increase in the paint booth (as was the case in the last example), the industrial engineering manager of Mole Industries proposes to invest $250,000 in the paint booth, but only to add sufficient automation to reduce operating expenses by $5,000 per month. The analysis is:

Product	Throughput per Minute	Constraint Usage (minutes)	Units Scheduled	Total Constraint Time	Total Throughput
1. Hedgehog Deluxe	$80	14	1,000	14,000	$1,120,000
2. Hedgehog Mini	70	20	500	10,000	700,000
3. Hedgehog Classic	65	40	200	8,000	520,000
4. Hedgehog Digger	42	10	688	6,880	288,960
		Total constraint scheduled time		38,880	
		Total constraint time available*		38,880	
			Total throughput		$2,628,960
			Total operating expenses		**2,395,000**
			Profit		**$233,960**
			Profit percentage		**8.7%**
			Investment		**$23,250,000**
			Annualized return on investment		**12.1%**

* Minutes per month = 30 days × 24 hours × 60 minutes × (1 − 0.10 maintenance time)

Changes were noted in bold. The investment creates a sufficient decline in total operating expenses to yield an increase in the annualized rate of return, to 12.1%. Consequently, this is a worthwhile investment opportunity.

Increase Upstream Capacity

There may be situations in which there is so little upstream capacity available that it takes an extremely long time to recover from an inventory buffer penetration. If so, the easiest way to justify an investment in the necessary sprint capacity is to calculate the amount of throughput being lost because of these buffer penetrations. The amount lost is then considered the throughput to be gained by making an investment. The following example illustrates the calculation.

EXAMPLE

Mole Industries has an old and cantankerous machine within one of its upstream workstations, which only operates within specifications on rare occasions. The production manager is extremely cheap, and wants to wait another year before investing in the $250,000 needed to replace the machine.

Because of the machine's extreme unreliability, the company has not been able to recover from a recent buffer penetration. If the machine were to be replaced, the buffer could be completely rebuilt in one month. At the moment, there is essentially no inventory buffer left, which has resulted in periodic shutdowns at the constraint for all jobs.

In the past month, the constraint has been nonoperational for 10% of the time, which equates to a reduction of $262,960 from the base case throughput level of $2,628,960. This means that the company could have purchased a replacement machine with the proceeds from somewhat less than one month of normal operations. In short, the old machine should be replaced as expeditiously as possible.

Increase Upstream Processing

The processing work performed at the constraint workstation may be comprised of several steps. If so, a possible constraint management option is to move one or more of these processing steps into a prior workstation upstream from the constraint, or even to create an entirely new workstation to handle the extra processing. Doing so can potentially free up a substantial amount of processing time at the constraint, which in turn can be used to generate more throughput.

The main decision points when investigating such a proposal are the incremental increase in cost to process the additional work upstream from the constraint, and the additional amount of throughput that will result from the change. The following example illustrates the concept.

EXAMPLE

The constraint workstation in the Mole Industries' production area involves a four-step configuration of a metal part. Further analysis of the situation reveals that the first of these steps could be handled by setting up a new workstation immediately in front of the inventory buffer. This workstation will require an investment of $150,000 for new equipment, as well as $30,000 per month in operating expenses. The result will be an immediate reduction in the constraint usage for each of the four products that Mole manufactures. The results are noted in the following model, where all changes from the base case are noted in bold.

Product	Throughput per Minute	Constraint Usage (minutes)	Units Scheduled	Total Constraint Time	Total Throughput**
1. Hedgehog Deluxe	$93.33	12	1,000	12,000	$1,120,000
2. Hedgehog Mini	77.78	18	500	9,000	700,000
3. Hedgehog Classic	76.47	34	200	6,800	520,000
4. Hedgehog Digger	52.50	8	1,385	11,080	581,700
		Total constraint scheduled time		38,880	
		Total constraint time available*		38,880	
				Total throughput	$2,921,700
				Total operating expenses	2,430,000
				Profit	$491,700
				Profit percentage	16.8%
				Investment	$23,150,000
				Annualized return on investment	25.5%

* Minutes per month = 30 days × 24 hours × 60 minutes × (1 − 0.10 maintenance time)
** Rounding is used for the throughput for the first three products listed in the table

In the model, the throughput per minute increases for all products, since the time required to process each item at the constraint decreases. This has no net effect on the total throughput generated by the first three products, but significantly increases the throughput of the fourth product, the Hedgehog Digger, since there is much more processing time available to manufacture additional units of this product. The result is a massive increase in total throughput in comparison to the increased operating expense, resulting in a large boost in both the profit percentage and the return on investment.

Outsource to a Supplier

One way to manage the constrained resource is to outsource work to keep some of the production burden away from the constraint. This option is always acceptable if the throughput generated by the outsourced products exceeds the price charged to the company by the supplier, *and* the company can replace the throughput per minute that was taken away from the constrained resource. The following example, which uses the basic constraint model as a baseline, illustrates the concept.

EXAMPLE

Mole Industries receives an offer from a supplier to outsource the Hedgehog Classic to it. The supplier will even drop ship the product to customers, so the product would no longer impact Mole's production process in any way. The downside of the offer is that the supplier's price is higher than the cost at which Mole can produce the Classic internally, so the total monthly throughput attributable to the Classic would decline by $300,000, from $520,000 to $220,000. However, there is a large customer order backlog for the Hedgehog Digger, so Mole could give increased production priority to the Digger instead. The analysis is as follows, with changes to the baseline model noted in bold.

Product	Throughput per Minute	Constraint Usage (minutes)	Units Scheduled	Total Constraint Time	Total Throughput
1. Hedgehog Deluxe	$80	14	1,000	14,000	$1,120,000
2. Hedgehog Mini	70	20	500	10,000	700,000
3. Hedgehog Classic	65	40	200	N/A	**220,000**
4. Hedgehog Digger	42	10	**1,488**	**14,880**	**624,960**
		Total constraint scheduled time		38,880	
		Total constraint time available*		38,880	
			Total throughput		**$2,664,960**
			Total operating expenses		2,400,000
			Profit		**$264,960**
			Profit percentage		**9.9%**
			Investment		$23,000,000
			Annualized return on investment		**13.8%**

* Minutes per month = 30 days × 24 hours × 60 minutes × (1 – 0.10 maintenance time)

Despite a large decline in throughput caused by the outsourcing deal, the company actually earns $36,000 more profit overall, because the Hedgehog Classic uses more of the constraint time per unit (40 minutes) than any other product; this allows the company to fill the available constraint time with 800 more Hedgehog Digger products, which require the smallest amount of constraint time per unit (10 minutes), and which generate sufficient additional throughput to easily offset the throughput decline caused by outsourcing. Mole Industries should accept the supplier's offer to outsource.

Summary

Constraint analysis is mostly used to review investment proposals in the production area, but can be used elsewhere. For example, there may be a bottleneck in the sales department if a salesperson insists on reviewing all quotes before they are released to customers, or if sales calls involve a demonstration by a sales technician, and there are too few of these technicians on staff. In these situations, constraint analysis can be highly effective.

Constraint analysis is an excellent tool for deciding whether a proposed investment does or does not increase the total throughput of a company. As such, it can flag a proposal as being not worthwhile, thereby forming an analysis threshold that can significantly reduce the number of valid proposals under consideration.

Chapter 6
Other Capital Budgeting Analyses

Introduction

In the previous chapters, we presented several discounted cash flow methods and constraint analysis as possible techniques for reviewing investment proposals. In this chapter, we continue with several other capital budgeting alternatives. The following analyses are usually not considered primary forms of analysis, but can be valuable additions to round out a thorough review of a proposed investment.

Breakeven Analysis

The breakeven point is the sales volume at which a project earns exactly no money. The concept can be used in the analysis of investment proposals to determine the minimum sales level at which an investment will earn a profit of zero. This information can be used to develop the minimum baseline of activity that a proposed project must achieve. Management can then use its best judgment to decide whether this minimum activity level can be met.

To calculate the breakeven point, divide total fixed expenses by the contribution margin. Contribution margin is sales minus all variable expenses, divided by sales. The formula is:

$$\frac{\text{Total fixed expenses}}{\text{Contribution margin percentage}}$$

EXAMPLE

Sheep Chops is a meat processing company that is contemplating the construction of a new meat packing facility for sheep, to be located in Wyoming. The facility is expected to incur $6,000,000 of annual labor and other costs. Labor costs only vary slightly with volume, since approximately the same number of employees are needed to staff the production line. In essence, this means that the entire operational cost of the facility is fixed. The current market price for an unprocessed lamb is $0.80 per pound, and the wholesale price for processed lamb is $2.00. This means that the contribution margin of the facility will be 60%, which is calculated as follows:

($2.00 Processed price - $0.80 Unprocessed price) ÷ $2.00 Processed price = 60%

Based on the contribution margin, the breakeven sales level is $10,000,000, which is calculated as follows:

$$\frac{\$6,000,000 \text{ Total fixed expenses}}{60\% \text{ Contribution margin percentage}}$$

$$= \$10,000,000 \text{ Breakeven sales level}$$

The current "most likely" scenario indicates that the facility can generate $12,000,000 of sales at current price points, which equates to profitability of $1,200,000, which is calculated as follows:

$$(\$12,000,000 \text{ Sales} \times 60\% \text{ Contribution margin}) - \$6,000,000 \text{ Fixed costs}$$

$$= \$1,200,000 \text{ Profit}$$

A further analysis of the situation indicates that a large proportion of the world's sheep products are being diverted to China to meet an increased demand for lamb chops in that country. This increases the scarcity of lamb products in the United States, which will likely keep prices high. Management elects to enter into long-term supply contracts with several ranchers, thereby locking in an assured supply for the next ten years. The assumption of high prices and the action taken to assure supplies places the company in a position to reap excellent cash flows from the new facility for a number of years.

The Payback Method

The simplest and least accurate capital expenditure evaluation technique is the payback method. This approach is still heavily used, because it provides a very fast "back of the envelope" calculation of how soon a company will earn back its investment. This means that it provides a rough measure of how long a company will have its investment at risk before earning back the original amount expended. Thus, it is a rough measure of risk. There are two ways to calculate the payback period, which are:

1. *Simplified.* Divide the total amount of an investment by the average resulting cash flow. This approach can yield an incorrect assessment, because a proposal with cash flows skewed far into the future can yield a payback period that differs substantially from when actual payback occurs.
2. *Manual calculation.* Manually deduct the forecasted positive cash flows from the initial investment amount from Year 1 forward, until the investment is paid back. This method is slower, but ensures a higher degree of accuracy.

A decision rule can be added to the payback calculation, where an investment is rejected if the payback period exceeds a certain threshold amount. For example, if a business has a three-year threshold for its investments, all proposed investments having paybacks longer than three years will be rejected.

EXAMPLE

Milagro Corporation's CFO has received a proposal from a manager, asking to spend $1,500,000 on equipment that will result in cash inflows in accordance with the following table:

Year	Cash Flow
1	+$150,000
2	+150,000
3	+200,000
4	+600,000
5	+900,000

The total cash flows over the five-year period are projected to be $2,000,000, which is an average of $400,000 per year. When divided into the $1,500,000 original investment, this results in a payback period of 3.75 years. However, the briefest perusal of the projected cash flows reveals that the flows are heavily weighted toward the far end of the time period, so the results of this calculation cannot be correct.

Instead, the CFO runs the calculation year by year, deducting the cash flows in each successive year from the remaining investment. The results of this calculation are:

Year	Cash Flow	Net Invested Cash
0		-$1,500,000
1	+$150,000	-1,350,000
2	+150,000	-1,200,000
3	+200,000	-1,000,000
4	+600,000	-400,000
5	+900,000	0

The table indicates that the real payback period is located somewhere between Year 4 and Year 5. There is $400,000 of investment yet to be paid back at the end of Year 4, and there is $900,000 of cash flow projected for Year 5. The CFO assumes the same monthly amount of cash flow in Year 5, which means that he can estimate final payback as being just short of 4.5 years.

The payback method is not overly accurate, does not provide any estimate of how profitable a project may be, and does not take account of the time value of money. Further, it ignores all cash flows occurring after the payback period has been achieved, so that it has a bias against longer-term projects. Nonetheless, its extreme simplicity makes it a perennial favorite in many companies.

Discounted Payback

The accuracy of the payback method can be improved by incorporating the time value of money into the cash flows expected in each future year, which is known as discounted payback. However, doing so increases the complexity of this analysis method. To apply the time value of money to the calculation, follow these steps:

1. Create a table in which is listed the expected cash outflow related to the investment in Year 0.
2. In the following lines of the table, enter the cash inflows expected from the investment in each subsequent year.
3. Multiply the expected annual cash inflows in each year in the table by the applicable discount rate, using the same interest rate for all of the periods in the table. No discount rate is applied to the initial investment, since it occurs at once.
4. Create a column on the far right side of the table that lists the cumulative discounted cash flow for each year. The calculation in this final column is to add back the discounted cash flow in each period to the remaining negative balance from the preceding period. The balance is initially negative because it includes the cash outflow to fund the project.
5. When the cumulative discounted cash flow becomes positive, the time period that has passed up until that point represents the payback period.

EXAMPLE

We will continue with the preceding example. Milagro has a cost of capital of 7%, so the present value factor for 7% (see the Discounted Cash Flow Analysis chapter) is included in the payback table, with the following results:

Year	Cash Flow	7% Present Value Factor	Cash Flow Present Value	Net Invested Cash
0				-$1,500,000
1	+$150,000	0.9346	+$140,190	-1,359,810
2	+150,000	0.8734	+131,010	-1,228,800
3	+200,000	0.8163	+163,260	-1,065,540
4	+600,000	0.7629	+457,740	-607,800
5	+900,000	0.7130	+641,700	-33,900

The discounted payback calculation reveals that the payback period will be slightly longer than the five years of cash flows presented in the manager's original proposal.

The concept of discounted payback does have some value, for it indicates the point in time at which the initial investment has been recouped on a discounted basis. If a project is still expected to have a significant useful life after this point has been reached, then there is ample opportunity for additional returns to be generated. Alternatively, if the discounted payback is late in the useful life of an investment, then there is a substantial risk that no positive returns will ever be generated. From this viewpoint, a project with (for example) a discounted payback of two years with two additional years remaining in its useful life could be a better investment than a project with a discounted payback of three years with one additional year remaining thereafter in its useful life.

Accounting Rate of Return

The accounting rate of return is the ratio of an investment's average annual profits to the amount invested in it. If the outcome exceeds a threshold value, then an investment is approved. The formula for the accounting rate of return is:

$$\frac{\text{Average annual accounting profit}}{\text{Initial investment}}$$

- Where the profit is calculated as the profit related to a proposed investment using all accruals and non-cash expenses. If the project involves cost reduction instead of earning a profit, then the numerator is the amount of cost savings generated by the investment.
- Where the initial investment is calculated as the fixed asset investment plus any change in working capital caused by the investment.

The result of the calculation is expressed as a percentage. Thus, if a company projects that it will earn an average annual profit of $70,000 on an initial investment of $1,000,000, then the project has an accounting rate of return of 7%.

There are several serious problems with the accounting rate of return concept, which are:

- *Time value of money.* The measure does not factor in the time value of money. Thus, if there is currently a high market interest rate, the time value of money could completely offset any profit reported by a project - but the accounting rate of return does incorporate this factor, so it clearly overstates the profitability of proposed projects.
- *Cash flow.* The measure is derived from the accounting income of a business, rather than its cash flows. There can be a substantial difference between the two, which can result in unusual outcomes when compared to a discounted cash flow analysis.
- *Time-based risk.* There is no consideration of the increased risk in the variability of forecasts that arises over a long period of time.

In short, the accounting rate of return is not by any means a perfect method for evaluating a capital project, and so should be used (if at all) only in concert with a number of other evaluation tools. This measure would be of the most use for reviewing short-term investments where the impact of the time value of money is reduced.

Real Options

Another way to review a capital expenditure decision is to examine the value embedded in different strategic alternatives. This concept is known as a *real option*, which refers to the decision options available for a tangible asset. Most businesses ignore the real option concept, instead choosing to construct a net present value analysis for a single possible outcome. Instead, use the concept to examine a whole range of outcomes related to an investment. For example, a traditional investment analysis in an oil refinery might use a single price per barrel of oil for the entire investment period, whereas the actual price of oil will likely fluctuate far outside of the initial estimated price point over the course of the investment, and will also vary among the different products that the refinery can manufacture. An analysis based on real options would instead focus on the range of profits and losses that may be encountered over the course of the investment period as the prices of oil and petroleum products change over time. This analysis might lead the manager of an oil refinery to repeatedly switch production among different octane grades of gasoline, to take advantage of variations in market prices. These decision points will alter the cash flows of a project.

A comprehensive real options analysis begins with a review of the risks to which a project will be subjected, and then models for each of these risks or combinations of risks. To continue with the preceding example, an investor in an oil refinery project could expand the scope of the analysis beyond the price of oil, to also encompass the risks of possible new environmental regulations on the facility, the possible downtime caused by a supply shutdown, and the risk of damage caused by a hurricane.

A logical outcome of real options analysis is to be more careful in placing large bets on a single likelihood of probability. Instead, it can make more sense to place a series of small bets on different outcomes, and then alter the portfolio of investments over time as more information about the various risks becomes available. Once the key risks have been resolved, the best investment is easier to discern, so that a "bet the bank" investment can be made. In essence, a series of small investments are made in the near future, which are the price paid in order to obtain better information concerning a larger investment to be made at a later date.

EXAMPLE

An agriculture company wants to develop a new crop strain for either wheat or barley, to be sold for export. The primary intended market is an area in which wheat is currently the preferred crop. The company estimates that it can generate a 20% return on investment by developing a new wheat variant at a cost of $30 million. Since wheat is already the primary type of crop being planted, the odds of success are high. However, if the company can successfully develop a barley variant at a total cost of $50 million, its projected profits are 50%. The key risk with the barley project is farmer acceptance. Given the high profits that could be derived from selling barley, the company makes a small initial $1 million investment in a pilot project. If the level of farmer acceptance appears reasonable, the company can then invest an additional $8 million for a further roll out of the concept, followed by additional expenditures for more extended rollouts.

This use of real options allows the company to invest a relatively small amount to test its assumptions regarding a possible alternative investment. If the test does not work, the company has only lost $1 million. If the test succeeds, the company can pursue an alternative that may ultimately yield far higher profits than the more assured investment in wheat.

The concept illustrated in the preceding example of placing a series of targeted bets can be expanded over an entire product life cycle. For example, if the pilot test for the barley variant works, the company could continue to develop options for the rollout of the product to farmers in other countries. The company may have identified certain parts of the world where cultural differences make it more or less likely that farmers will convert their fields to barley production. Accordingly, the company can invest in a target area in each of these geographic regions to measure acceptance levels, and then either proceed with a full-scale product rollout or withdraw from the market entirely. The following graphic illustrates how the process might work.

Real Options Rollout Plan for Barley Product

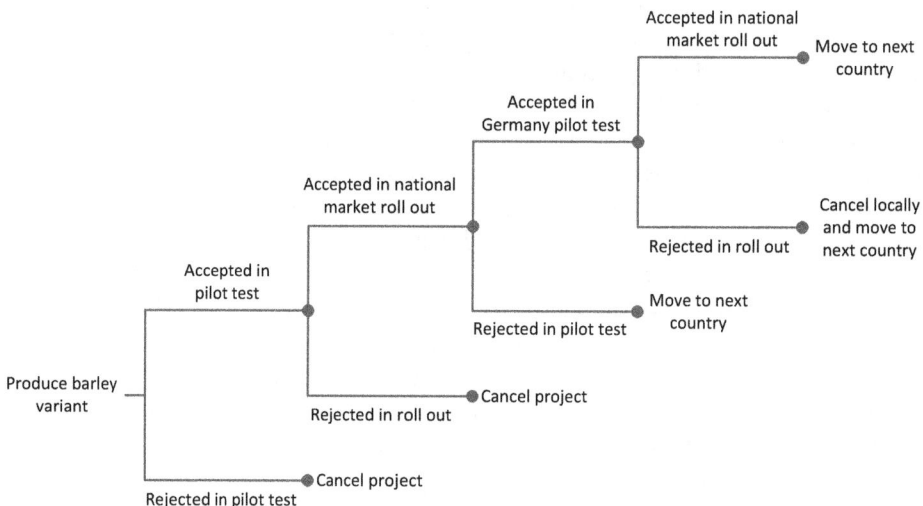

The options concept can also be used to delay a project. For example, if there is a downturn in demand or in unit prices, it can make sense to stop investing in new production capacity until market conditions are more favorable. In this case, a business is using its investment-to-date as the cost of an option that allows it to jump back into the market on short notice if conditions improve. Similarly, a real estate investor could purchase an option to buy property at a specific price and over a designated period of time. If the value of the property increases, the investor exercises the option and buys the property, earning a profit on the increase in value. If the property value does not increase, the investor lets the option expire.

Options analysis can also be used to structure the manner in which a business enters into a new market. For example, if there is uncertainty about the level of demand that will exist for a new product, a pilot plant might be constructed that is designed to have a relatively short useful life. By doing so, the investment in the new market is minimized, and the facility can be disassembled and its components sold off if demand does not materialize.

A concern with using real options is that competitors may be using the same concept at the same time, and may use the placing of small bets to arrive at the same conclusions as the company. The result can be that several competitors will enter a market at approximately the same time, driving down the initially rich margins that management may have assumed were associated with a real option. Thus, the parameters of real options constantly change, and so must be re-evaluated at regular intervals.

Another concern relates to the last point that competitors may jump into the same market. This means that a business cannot evaluate the results of its options analyses in a leisurely manner. Instead, each option must be evaluated quickly and decisions made to make additional investments (or not) before the competition gets a jump on the situation.

The Outsourcing Decision

It may be possible to avoid a capital purchase entirely by outsourcing the work to which it is related. By doing so, a company may be able to eliminate all assets related to the area (rather than acquiring more assets), while the burden of maintaining a sufficient asset base now shifts to the supplier. The supplier may even buy the company's assets related to the area being outsourced. This situation is a well-established alternative for high technology manufacturing, as well as for information technology services, but is likely not viable outside of these areas.

If there is an outsourcing opportunity, the cash flows resulting from doing so could be highly favorable for the first few years, as capital expenditures vanish. However, the supplier must also earn a profit and pay for its own infrastructure, so the cost over the long term will probably not vary dramatically from what a company would have experienced if it had kept a functional area in-house. There are three exceptions that can bring about a long-term cost reduction. They are:

- *Excess capacity.* A supplier may have such a large amount of excess capacity already that it does not need to invest further for some time, thereby potentially depressing the costs that it would otherwise pass through to its customers. However, this excess capacity pool will eventually dry up, so it tends to be a short-term anomaly.
- *High volume.* There are some outsourcing situations where the supplier is handling such a massive volume of activity from multiple customers that its costs on a per-unit basis decline below the costs that a company could ever achieve on its own. This situation can yield long-term savings to a company.
- *Low costs.* A supplier may locate its facility and work force in low-cost countries or regions within countries. This can yield significant cost reductions in the short term, but as many suppliers use the same technique, it is driving up costs in all parts of the world. Thus, this cost disparity is useful for a period of time, but is gradually declining as a long-term option.

There are risks involved in shifting functions to suppliers. First, a supplier may go out of business, leaving the company scrambling to shift work to a new supplier. Second, a supplier may gradually ramp up prices to the point where the company is substantially worse off than if it had kept the function in-house. Third, the company may have so completely purged the outsourced function from its own operations that it is now completely dependent on the supplier, and has no ability to take it back in-house. Fourth, the supplier's service level may decline to the point where it is impairing the ability of the company to operate. And finally, the company may have entered into a multi-year deal, and cannot escape from the contract if the business arrangement does not work out. These are significant issues, and must be weighed as part of the outsourcing decision.

The cautions noted here about outsourcing do not mean that it should be avoided as an option. On the contrary, a rapidly growing company that has minimal access to funds may cheerfully hand off multiple operations to suppliers in order to avoid the up-front costs associated with those operations. Outsourcing is less attractive to stable, well-established companies that have better access to capital.

In summary, outsourcing is an attractive option for rapidly growing companies that do not have sufficient cash to pay for capital expenditures, but also carries with it a variety of risks involving shifting key functions to a supplier over which a company may not have a great deal of control.

Research and Development Funding Analysis

The funding process for research and development (R&D) projects tends to result in the funding of less-risky projects. The reason is that there is usually not enough cash available to fund all proposed projects, so a ranking system must be imposed to determine which projects will receive funding. The ranking is driven by a discounted cash flows analysis, for which a higher discount rate is imposed on the riskier projects. Since this analysis tends to reduce the cash flows associated with riskier projects, only safer R&D projects are funded. The typical result is that a business pours more cash into the extension of its existing product lines, which are considered safe investments, and little cash into real innovation.

One way to break through this safety-driven selection process is to deliberately allocate cash to several classifications of R&D projects, of which one is for high-risk endeavors. The amount allocated to each classification will vary, depending on management's willingness to lose money on high-risk projects. In general, this concept will increase the probability that a business will come up with a breakthrough product that can lead to an entirely new product line.

When cash is deliberately invested in high-risk R&D projects, there will inevitably be a number of project failures, either because the results will not be commercially viable or because the project is an outright failure. The real problem is when there are *few* failures, because it indicates that the company is not investing in sufficiently risky projects, with their attendant high returns.

To determine the amount of project failure being experienced, summarize the total expense related to projects that have been cancelled (known as *R&D waste*). While this metric can be deliberately altered by delaying the date on which a project is cancelled, it can still provide relevant input into the amount of project risk being incurred over multiple periods.

Even when the allocation of funding into different classifications increases the odds of funding a riskier R&D project, it is still necessary to allocate funds *within* each classification. A possible approach for deciding between projects is to use *expected commercial value* (ECV), which amalgamates the probabilities of success into a more standard net present value calculation. The formula is:

(((Project net present value × probability of commercial success) – commercialization cost) × (probability of technical success)) – product development cost

---

EXAMPLE

Entwhistle Electric is considering an investment in a tiny battery for cell phone applications. There is some risk that the battery cannot be developed in the necessary size. Facts pertaining to the project are:

Project net present value	$8,000,000
Probability of commercial success	90%
Commercialization cost	$1,500,000
Probability of technical success	75%
Product development cost	$3,500,000

Entwhistle's financial analyst derives the following ECV for the project from the preceding information:

((($8,000,000 Project NPV × 90% probability of commercial success) – $1,500,000 commercialization cost)

× (75% probability of technical success)) – $3,500,000 product development cost

Expected commercial value = $775,000

An ECV analysis will inevitably result in some projects not being funded. However, not being funded does not necessarily equate to being permanently cancelled. These projects might become more tempting prospects for funding at a later date, depending on changes in such areas as:

- Competitor actions
- Legal liability
- Price points for adjacent products
- Raw materials availability
- Technical advances

Because of these issues, it may make sense to schedule an occasional review of projects that have failed the ECV test, to see if circumstances now make them worthy of an investment.

Complex Systems Analysis

When analyzing a possible investment, it is useful to also analyze the system into which the investment will be inserted. If the system is unusually complex, it is likely to take longer for the new asset to function as expected within the system. The reason for the delay is that there may be unintended consequences that ripple through the system, requiring adjustments in multiple areas that must be addressed before any gains from the initial investment can be achieved.

It may initially appear that the multitude of factors to consider in a complex system can be accounted for by creating an equally complex analysis model. However, virtually all models, no matter how complex, are not entirely complete; there are always additional factors that have not been considered that can impact a model in unexpected ways. Further, some factors may interact in unexpected ways, resulting in outcomes that are well outside of what might be expected.

EXAMPLE

ABC Airlines is modeling whether to offer its customers a new route into Denver from Kansas City. ABC must consider a number of factors that can impact flight service, such as the impact of snowfall on the number of travelers to the area's ski resorts, whether a new high-speed train from Kansas City to Denver will impact the number of paying passengers, the extent to which upstart low-cost airlines may drive down prices, and how the price of aviation fuel will drive up ticket prices. ABC elects not to provide service, after which the International Olympic Committee grants Denver the next Winter Olympics, which triggers an upsurge in travel even in advance of the games. Thus, an outlier event arises that would not normally have been factored into the decision, but which has an impact on the decision.

A basic rule of investing in a complex environment is that it is impossible to understand the full impact of the investment. There may be any number of adjustments required that will call for additional investments of both time and money. Consequently, the more complex the environment, the more time and money should be allocated to an investment, even if there may not appear to be any immediate need for the additional investment.

Summary

This chapter has presented a mix of analysis techniques and additional issues to consider when deciding what to do with an investment proposal. The breakeven point, payback period, and accounting rate of return can be used to develop additional insights into a proposed use of funds. The real options, outsourcing, and R&D funding concepts can be used to explore alternative ways in which to make an investment. The discussion of complex systems provides a general warning regarding the level of complexity that may be encountered when dealing with investment proposals.

Chapter 7
The Lease or Buy Decision

Introduction

After a company makes the decision to acquire an asset, it must decide how to finance the purchase. A common decision is whether to buy the asset with cash or to lease it. A lease is an arrangement where the lessor agrees to allow the lessee to use an asset for a stated period of time in exchange for a series of fixed payments. The arrangement typically requires that the asset be returned after a stated interval, though the lessee may have the option to extend the lease or buy the asset at the end of the lease term. In this chapter, we discuss the nature of the lease or buy comparison, the circumstances under which leasing is a beneficial alternative, and the lease terms that can potentially increase the cost of a lease.

The Lease or Buy Decision

There are a multitude of factors that a lessor includes in the formulation of the monthly rate that it charges, such as the down payment, the residual value of the asset at the end of the lease, and the interest rate, which makes it difficult to break out and examine each element of the lease. Instead, it is much easier to create separate net present value tables for the lease and buy alternatives, and then compare the results of the two tables to see which alternative is better from a cash flow perspective. The following example illustrates the use of net present value for this analysis.

EXAMPLE

Milford Sound is contemplating the purchase of an asset for $500,000. It can buy the asset outright, or do so with a lease. Its cost of capital is 8%, and its incremental income tax rate is 21%. The following two tables show the net present values of both options.

Buy Option

Year	Depreciation	Income Tax Savings (21%)	Discount Factor (8%)	Net Present Value
0				-$500,000
1	$100,000	$21,000	0.9259	19,444
2	100,000	21,000	0.8573	18,003
3	100,000	21,000	0.7938	16,670
4	100,000	21,000	0.7350	15,435
5	100,000	21,000	0.6806	14,297
Totals	$500,000	$105,000		**$416,151**

Lease Option

Year	Pretax Lease Payments	Income Tax Savings (21%)	After-Tax Lease Cost	Discount Factor (8%)	Net Present Value
1	$135,000	$28,350	$106,650	0.9259	$98,747
2	135,000	28,350	106,650	0.8573	91,431
3	135,000	28,350	106,650	0.7938	84,659
4	135,000	28,350	106,650	0.7350	78,388
5	135,000	28,350	106,650	0.6806	72,586
Totals	$675,000	$141,750	$533,250		$425,811

Thus, the net purchase cost of the buy option is $416,151, while the net purchase cost of the lease option is $425,811. The buy option involves the lowest cash outflow for Milford, and so is the better option.

Leasing Concerns

There is an undeniable attraction to acquiring assets with a lease, since it replaces a large up-front cash outflow with a series of monthly payments. However, before signing a lease agreement, be aware of the following issues that can increase the cost of the arrangement:

- *Buyout price.* Many leases include an end-of-lease buyout price that is inordinately high. If the lessee wants to continue using a leased asset, the buyout price may be so outrageous that the only realistic alternative is to continue making lease payments, which generates outsized profits for the lessor. Therefore, always negotiate the size of the buyout payment before signing a lease agreement. If the buyout is stated as the "fair market value" of the asset at the end of the lease term, the amount can be subject to interpretation, so include a clause that allows for arbitration to determine the amount of fair market value.
- *Deposit.* The lessor may require that an inordinately large deposit be made at the beginning of the lease term, from which the lessor can then earn interest over the term of the lease.
- *Deposit usage.* The terms of a lease may allow the lessor to charge any number of fees against the up-front deposit made by the lessee, resulting in little of the deposit being returned at the end of the lease.
- *Lease fee.* The lessor may charge a lease fee, which is essentially a paperwork charge to originate the lease. It may be possible to reduce or eliminate this fee.
- *Rate changes.* The lessor may offer a low lease rate during the beginning periods of a lease, and then escalate the rates later in the lease term. Be sure to calculate the average lease rate to see if the implicit interest rate is reasonable.

In these sorts of arrangements, a rate ramp-up usually indicates an average interest rate that is too high.

- *Return fees.* When the lease term is over, the lessor may require that the leased asset be shipped at the lessee's cost to a distant location, and sometimes even in the original packaging.

- *Termination notification.* The lease agreement may require the lessee to notify the lessor in writing that it intends to terminate the lease as of the termination date stated in the contract. If the lessee does not issue this notification in a timely manner, it is obligated to continue leasing the asset, or to pay a large termination fee. Whenever this clause appears in a lease agreement, always negotiate it down to the smallest possible termination notification period.

- *Wear-and-tear standards.* A lease agreement may contain unreasonable standards for assigning a high rate of wear-and-tear to leased assets when they have been returned to the lessor, resulting in additional fees being charged to the lessee.

In short, many lessors rely upon obfuscation of the lease terms to generate a profit, so it makes sense to delve into every clause in a lease agreement and to be willing to bargain hard for changes to the terms. Also, have a well-managed system in place for retaining lease agreements and monitoring when the key dates associated with each lease will arise. Finally, conduct a cost review after each lease agreement has been terminated, to determine the total out-of-pocket cost and implicit interest rate; the result may be the discovery that certain lessors routinely gouge the company, and should not be used again.

In addition to the issues just noted, the lessee also loses access to any favorable changes in the residual value of leased assets, since the lessor usually retains ownership of the assets. Also, the lessee cannot take advantage of the tax benefits of depreciation when a lease is classified as an operating lease; instead, the lessor records the depreciation and takes advantage of the related tax benefits. This latter issue may not be a concern if the lessee has minimal taxable income that could be reduced by a depreciation charge, and does not expect to be able to use a net operating loss carryforward in future years.

The list of concerns with leasing arrangements may appear formidable. However, they also have a number of advantages, as explained in the next section.

Leasing Advantages

The leasing concerns just described should introduce a note of caution into dealings with lessors, since a careful analysis of lease terms may reveal an inordinately high cost. However, there are also a number of advantages to leasing, which include:

- *Asset servicing.* The lessor may have a sophisticated asset servicing capability. Though the cost of this servicing may be high, it can result in fast servicing intervals and therefore extremely high equipment usage levels. In some cases, the presence of a servicing capability may be the main attraction of a leasing deal.

- *Competitive lease rates*. A lessor can offer quite competitive lease rates. This situation arises when a lessor buys assets in such high volumes that it can obtain volume purchase discounts from suppliers, some of which it may pass along to lessees. The lessor may also be able to borrow funds at a lower rate than the lessee, and can share some of the cost differential.

- *Financing accessibility*. A lessor is more likely to enter into a leasing arrangement with a company that is experiencing low profitability than a traditional lender. This is because the leased asset is collateral for the lessor, which can take the asset back if the lessee is unable to continue making timely lease payments. Conversely, a traditional lender might have a considerably more difficult time accessing company assets, and so would be less inclined to lend funds for the purchase of assets.

- *New technology*. A non-monetary advantage of leasing is that a company is continually swapping out old equipment for newer and more technologically advanced equipment. This can present a competitive advantage in those cases where the equipment is being used within a core function, or used to enhance products or services.

- *Off-balance sheet transaction*. Depending on the terms of a leasing arrangement, it may be possible for a lessee to avoid having to state its remaining lease payment liabilities on its balance sheet. By doing so, the balance sheet shows the company as having fewer obligations than is really the case, and so the business appears more solvent. However, it may still be necessary to reveal the annual amount of future lease payments in the accompanying financial statement disclosures.

- *Reserve available debt*. The company can reserve room on its existing line of credit by instead using a lease to buy an asset.

- *Short-term usage*. A leasing arrangement can be an effective alternative for those assets that are expected to have little value by the end of their lease terms, or for which the company expects to install a replacement asset at about the time of the lease termination.

Summary

We have spent a large proportion of this chapter addressing the ways in which a lease can turn sour, due to terms that may be hidden deep within a lease agreement. Though the result can be an inordinately high financing cost, leasing can still prove to be an excellent alternative to buying assets outright. The keys to a successful leasing deal are to be aware of the situations in which leasing makes the most sense, reviewing lease terms with great care before signing an agreement, and complying with all lease terms.

Chapter 8
Capital Budgeting Controls

Introduction

Capital budgeting can involve the expenditure of massive amounts of cash, to the point where an incorrect or unauthorized expenditure could bankrupt a business. Consequently, it is mandatory to weave a comprehensive set of controls into the capital budgeting process, so that expenditures are only made after due consideration and analysis. A number of controls are described in this chapter.

Capital Budgeting Controls

The key focus of controls for the acquisition of key assets is to ensure that the company needs the assets. This means that controls are designed to require an evaluation of how a proposed investment will fit into the company's operations, and what kind of return on investment it will generate. A secondary set of controls are also needed to ensure that all acquisition transactions are forced to follow this review process. With these goals in mind, consider using the following controls:

- *Require an approval form.* There should be an approval form that requires an applicant to describe the investment, how it is to be used, and the return on investment that will be generated (if any). This standardizes the information about each proposal, and also provides a handy signature form for various approvals.

> **Associated Policy:** There should be a corporate policy that requires the submission of an approval form for any investment request. A sample policy is: *Employees must submit a capital budgeting request for any purchase exceeding the corporate capitalization limit.*

- *Require independent analysis of the approval form.* Someone who is skilled in proposal analysis should review each submitted approval form. This analysis includes a verification that all supporting documents are attached to the form, that all assumptions are reasonable, and that the conclusions reached appear to be valid. The person conducting this analysis does not necessarily render an opinion on whether to make an investment, but should point out any flaws in the proposal. This person should *not* report to the person who submitted the proposal, since that would be a conflict of interest.
- *Require multi-level approvals for more expensive investments.* If an investment proposal is *really* expensive, impose a requirement for a number of approvals by people in positions of increasing levels of authority. Though

clearly time-consuming, the intent is to make a number of people aware of the request, so that the organization as a whole will be absolutely sure of its position before allowing a purchase to proceed.

- *Focus more attention on rush requests.* Someone may try to avoid the usual review steps in order to make an investment right now on a rush basis. These are precisely the sorts of situations where it may make sense to impose a tighter review, since the rush nature of the purchase may be keeping people from due deliberation of the alternatives available. The exact nature of this control will vary under the circumstances, but the key point is to not eliminate *all* reviews and approvals just because someone says that an investment must be made at once.
- *Impose a mandatory waiting period.* Though controversial, it may make sense to impose a waiting period before an investment is made, on the grounds that due deliberation may reveal that some items are simply not needed, and so should not be bought. Taken to extremes, such a control can result in an excessively plodding organization, so use it with care.
- *Do not issue a purchase order without a signed approval form.* Train the purchasing staff to not order fixed assets unless the requestor has a signed approval form. Better yet, route all such purchase orders to a senior executive, such as the chief financial officer, for approval.
- *Assign a monitoring cost accountant.* For a really large project, there should be a designated person who is responsible for tracking the costs accumulating against the project, and reporting this information to management. This person also decides when to shift a project out of the construction-in-progress account and into a regular fixed asset classification. The ideal person for this task is a cost accountant, since this position is trained in cost accumulation and analysis.
- *Conduct milestone reviews.* For longer-term asset installations, there should be a series of milestone events at which the management team responsible for the project examines expenditures to date, progress on the project, and any issues relating to the remaining tasks to be completed. Though rare, the team may occasionally use the information obtained in this review to cancel a project entirely. A more common response is a variety of adjustments to improve the odds of successful completion within the cost budget.
- *Conduct post-installation reviews.* An analyst or cost accountant should examine the results of an investment after it has been installed and its cash flow impact can be projected. Though this is an after-the-fact detective control, it is still useful for spotting erroneous information in investment proposals or bad decisions related to them, which can then be addressed in new investment proposals.

> **Associated Policy:** A policy can be used as the basis for examining completed capital projects. For example: *The results of all capital purchases in excess of $___ shall be reviewed and reported to management within __ months of final installation.*

The controls noted here will absolutely slow down the capital budgeting process, and with good reason – part of their intent is to encourage more deliberation about why an investment is being made. Nonetheless, these controls will appear onerous to those people trying to make investments that are relatively inexpensive, so it is certainly acceptable to adopt a reduced set of controls for such items, perhaps simply treating them as accounts payable that require a single approval signature on a purchase order.

Similarly, one can consider a more streamlined set of controls for investments that must be made at once. However, keep in mind that some managers intent on subverting the system of controls can characterize *everything* as a rush requirement, just to avoid the usual reviews and approvals. Consequently, if a reduced set of controls is adopted for such investments, at least conduct an after-the-fact review of the circumstances of these purchases, to see if the reduced controls were actually justified.

Summary

Capital budgeting controls essentially involve forms and approvals, both of which require the active use of employee training concerning the use of forms and how to obtain approvals. Thus, proper attention to initial and ongoing training is essential to maintaining control over capital budgeting.

Glossary

C

Capital budgeting. The process of deciding whether to invest in fixed assets or activities.

Capital expenditure. Funds used to acquired fixed assets.

Capital lease. A leasing arrangement where the lessee is effectively taking ownership of an asset.

Capital rationing. The process used to allocate limited funds to investment proposals.

Cash flow. The net amount of cash that a business receives or disburses over a period of time.

Constraint. A bottleneck that restricts the level of output from a system.

Cost of capital. The blended cost of a firm's debt, preferred stock, and equity.

D

Depreciation. A non-cash expense that reduces the amount of an asset over its useful life.

Discount rate. The interest rate at which future dollars are reduced to their present value.

I

Interest. The cost to borrow funds.

Internal rate of return. The rate of return at which the aggregate present values of a set of future cash inflows and outflows equals zero.

L

Lease. An arrangement where a lessor allows a lessee to use·an asset for a period of time in exchange for a series of fixed payments.

Line of credit. A commitment from a lender to pay a borrower whenever it needs cash, up to a pre-set maximum level.

Local optimization. The practice of improving the efficiency of all operations, even though the net impact does not improve the overall performance of the entity.

N

Net present value. The net difference between the present value of cash inflows and cash outflows associated with an investment.

O

Operating expenses. All company expenses other than totally variable costs.

Operating lease. A leasing arrangement where the lessor retains ownership of the leased asset.

R

Real option. The decision options available for a tangible asset.

T

Tax shield. The use of interest expense to offset taxable income.

Terminal value. The aggregated cash flows for the period beyond which detailed cash flows are being predicted.

Throughput. Revenues minus totally variable expenses.

Time value of money. The concept that invested money can earn a return.

W

Working capital. Current assets minus current liabilities.

Index

www.ingramcontent.com/pod-product-compliance
Lightning Source LLC
Chambersburg PA
CBHW061126210326
41518CB00033B/2449

* 9 7 8 1 6 4 2 2 1 2 9 3 8 *